Authentic

DISCIPLE OF JESUS

1 John 3:18

Todd Tomasella

Authentic Disciple of Jesus

All Scripture quotations deliberately taken from the Authorized Version of the Holy Bible, the King James Version

ISBN: 9798502162807

Visit: SafeGuardYourSoul.com

Email: info@safeguardyoursoul.com

Mailing Address:
Todd Tomasella
9201 Warren Pkwy. Ste. 200
Frisco, Texas 75035

Printed in the United States of America

"My little children, let us not love in word, neither in tongue; but in deed and in truth."

1 John 3:18

Note from the Author

It is the author's hope, desire, and prayer, that the LORD will bless the reader with the deep desire for authenticity as He alone can do. Having grown up "religious," after being saved, this disciple was convicted to begin praying to the LORD to purge and strip away every trace of falsity, fakery, and plastic self-righteousness, and to make him whole according to His will. To this day the prayer is: *Dear Father, in Jesus' Name, please purify my heart and life of every vestige, every trace of religiosity and establish this servant in Your bless-ed authenticity – as Your authentic disciple.*

Table of Contents

Chapter 1

Authentic Joy

"All the days of the afflicted are evil: but <u>he that is of a merry heart hath a continual feast</u>." Proverbs 15:15

True joy which comes forth out of an abiding fellowship with Christ, yields the fruit of **"a continual feast,"** no matter what hardships or difficult seasons of trials may come.

> **"My brethren, count it all joy when ye fall into divers temptations; [3] Knowing this, that the trying of your faith worketh patience. [4] But let patience have her perfect work, that ye may be perfect and entire, wanting nothing." James 1:2-4**

Is **"a continual feast"** possible at all times and through all seasons in every difficulty? Yes, and the key is keeping God's Word running rich in your life—ingesting it, meditating upon it, memorizing it and sharing it!

> **"So they read in the book in the law of God distinctly, and gave the sense, and caused them to understand the reading. [9] And**

Nehemiah, which is the Tirshatha, and Ezra the priest the scribe, and the Levites that taught the people, said unto all the people, This day is holy unto the LORD your God; mourn not, nor weep. For all the people wept, when they heard the words of the law. [10] Then he said unto them, Go your way, eat the fat, and drink the sweet, and send portions unto them for whom nothing is prepared: for this day is holy unto our Lord: neither be ye sorry; <u>for the joy of the LORD is your strength</u>." Nehemiah 8:8-10

What's the context and condition to be met for the joy of the LORD to fill our hearts and be the strength of our daily lives? If we are low spiritually, it could only be for one reason—we didn't stay filled with the Spirit and the Word. Dear disciple of Jesus, the LORD would have you to get filled! Stay filled! Overflow!

"<u>Let the word of Christ dwell in you richly</u> *(abundantly)* in all wisdom; teaching and admonishing one another in psalms and hymns and spiritual songs, singing with grace in your hearts to the Lord." Colossians 3:16

Getting into and remaining in God's Word daily is essential for enduring to the end, continuing, abiding in Christ (Matthew 25:1-13).

"Blessed are they which do hunger and thirst after righteousness: for they shall be filled." Matthew 5:6

Pessimism, glass half full, whining, complaining, etc., comes out of a darkened heart that is in utter need of the light of Christ. **"He that hath a froward heart findeth no good: and he that hath a perverse tongue falleth into mischief"** (Proverbs 17:20).

The wicked-hearted person does not seek the LORD, and is therefore void of His presence, His joy, His love, His faith, His grace, and so finds nothing to be thankful for.

Depression Cannot Exist in a Singing Saint!

"Behold, my servants shall sing for joy of heart." Isaiah 65:14

"By him therefore let us offer the sacrifice of praise to God continually, that is, the

fruit of our lips giving thanks to his name." Hebrews 13:15

"Rejoice in the Lord alway: and again I say, Rejoice." Philippians 4:4

When you are continually feasting on the bless-ed bountiful banquet of the LORD's table, gratefully praising His holy name, merriment will fill your heart and His divine glory your face. Are you ready to experience a **"continual feast"**?

"Glory ye in his holy name: let the heart of them rejoice that seek the LORD. [11] Seek the LORD and his strength, seek his face continually." 1 Chronicles 16:10-11

Jesus makes us shine from the inside out—and it doesn't matter what we're enduring! Divine joy is our **"strength"** (Nehemiah 8:10).

When we are blessed to be placed into the desert, in the valley for a season, having no place to look but upward, our praying and study of God's Word ceases to be a mere formality and becomes a groaning and a crying out to the LORD in deep rooted desperation and fervency.

There's no such thing as a person who is full of joy and not in the Word.

Often in the fake "prophetic" or "word of faith" houses of wickedness, we see the minister calling people up so they can pray for those in depression to have joy. Is this biblical?

Where in the Word, do we see Christ or any prophet or apostle or anyone in the early church praying for depression to leave someone? OR even that someone will have joy? JOY is a fruit produced only via obedience and not because someone prays for it (Galatians 5:22-23).

Are we denying that depression exists? No. In the Word we see people like the prophet Elijah getting depressed, right? See 1 Kings 19:4. Is replacing depression with the JOY of the LORD God's will? Yes, yet how do we see this happen by getting in God's Word?

You see, false ministries identify problems yet make themselves the solution instead of instructing you to personally get into the Word so the Word will get into you—to personally **"STUDY to shew"** YOURSELF approved unto God (2 Timothy 2:15).

And guess what happens when the individual repents and seeks God for himself in God's Word? ALL other problems are solved! Yet those **"false teachers"** and **"false prophets"** among us who make merchandise of you, want you to be their return customers (2 Peter 2:1-3).

Everyone desires the joy of the LORD, right? Yes, yet only those who are willing to devour His Word to get it into their hearts and keep it flowing into their hearts, will experience that great joy of the LORD which is our strength! In context, the joy of the LORD is the strength of those who read it, hear it, embrace it, and keep it flowing into their mind and heart daily! Read Nehemiah 8:8-10.

The Bible reveals that joy comes in the MOURNING and with the ingestion of the written WORD! (See Psalms 30:5; Ecclesiastes 7:2-5; Jeremiah 15:16.) Got depression? Good, get with God in fresh repentance and get lost in HIS WORD! Cry out to Jesus for yourself!

You want JOY to replace your depression? Good. Now repent and get in the Word and the Word will get into you and will be **"the JOY and REJOICING"** of your heart—which means all depression will be vanquished! STOP praying for people's depression and start directing them to get into the Word so the WORD can get into them. Exhort them to drink the healing oil of God's WORD.

God's Word cannot get into us until we get into it!

Fueling the Joy of the LORD

The divine fuel of joy is God's Word. No fuel = No joy. When the Word of God is ingested daily, consistently and continually, joy that's on the inside, shining on the outside, is the result!

> **"Thy words were found, and I did eat them; and thy word was unto me the joy and rejoicing of mine heart: for I am called by thy name, O LORD God of hosts." Jeremiah 15:16**

The daily cross—putting God first and not self—is essential to being consumed with the joy of the LORD.

"But seek ye first the kingdom of God, and his righteousness; and all these things shall be added unto you" (Matthew 6:33). Putting God first assures that His divine blessing will rest upon our lives.

When we are full of misery it's because we're still full of self instead of being full of God (John 3:30; Philippians 2). **"Man that is born of a woman is of few days, and full of trouble"** (Job 14:1).

How can we possibly be full of the joy of Jesus if we are still full of sinful self? When we relinquish the control of our lives to the One who made us, His joy and His blessing fills our lives.

There's no need to walk around **"troubled"** when in fact you are a **"new creature,"** a regenerated ambassador of Christ, filled with His love, walking in His truth.

> **"Therefore if any man be in Christ, he is a new creature: old things are passed away; behold, all things are become new. [18] And all things are of God, who hath reconciled us to himself by Jesus Christ, and hath given to us the ministry of reconciliation;" 2 Corinthians 5:17-18**

As a born-again believer you are **"predestinate*(d)* to be conformed to the image of his Son"** (Romans 8:29). When the crucified image of His Son Jesus is at work in our personal lives, the resurrection glory of Christ is reciprocally raising us upward.

> **"Always bearing about in the body the dying of the Lord Jesus, that the life also of Jesus might be made manifest in our body. [11] For we which live are alway delivered unto death for Jesus' sake, that the life also of Jesus might be made manifest in our mortal flesh. [12] So then death worketh in us, but life in you." 2 Corinthians 4:10-12**

The crucifixion of the self-life, the strippings, the emptying of self, taking on the nature and mission of Christ to love others, is paramount to walking in the mind of Christ and having a **"continual feast."**

The stripping away of the **"old man"** nature of self is the same as the circumcision of the heart (Romans 2:28-29; Philippians 3:3; Colossians 2:11-12).

Reading Philippians 2 on a regular basis will be most significant.

If we've not yet been reduced to rags (the realization of our own filthy rags), be aware that our LORD loves us too much to leave us as we are and has ordained the allowance of seasons of suffering in order to bring us to utter contrition.

> **"The LORD is nigh unto them that are of a broken heart; and saveth such as be of a contrite spirit." Psalms 34:18**

> **"The sacrifices of God are a broken spirit: a broken and a contrite heart, O God, thou wilt not despise." Psalms 51:17**

The cup or the vessel consumed and filled by the Holy Spirit through the cross life is going to overflow onto others perpetually. As long as we are emptied of self and full of the Holy Spirit, the overflowing blessings of God will be working in our lives. That's ministry—flowing in and through God's people.

> **"Thou preparest a table before me in the presence of mine enemies: thou anointest my head with oil; my cup runneth over." Psalms 23:5**

> **"Nevertheless when it** *(the heart)* **shall turn to the Lord, the vail shall be taken away. [17] Now the Lord is that Spirit: and where the Spirit of the Lord is, there is liberty. [18] But we all, with open face beholding as in a**

glass the glory of the Lord, are changed into the same image from glory to glory, even as by the Spirit of the Lord." 2 Corinthians 3:16-18

"Let your light so shine before men, that they may see your good works, and glorify your Father which is in heaven." Matthew 5:16

The Joy of the LORD and the Cross

The yielding of the **"fruit of the Spirit"** (Galatians 5:22) comes out of the resurrection life of Christ in the crucified saint.

The only way to live from a position of resurrection divine strength and the light of Christ is to live the crucified life—where you are dead and buried and Christ is perpetually, reciprocally raising you upward! Read 2 Corinthians 4:10-12; Galatians 2:20; 5:24; 6:14.

IF we are not obediently, aggressively, decidedly, absolutely crucifying the flesh, the flesh is controlling us and is crucifying Christ right out of our lives (Romans 8:5-14). There is no middle ground (Matthew 6:24; 12:30; 1 Corinthians 10:21). Those who procrastinate and have this notion that in the future they are going to get around to laying down their life for real, fasting and praying, and dying to self, are under the powers of darkness. Notice in Galatians 5:24 the word **"HAVE." "And they that are Christ's <u>have</u> crucified the flesh with the affections and lusts"** (Galatians 5:24).

Fasting is a type of self-inflicted crucifixion of the flesh, putting to death the self-life, in compliance with the stated will of God—the command of God to deny self, take up the cross, and follow Christ (Luke 9:23-24).

> *"And they that are Christ's - True believers in him. Have thus crucified the flesh - Nailed it, as it were, to a cross whence it has no power to break loose but is continually weaker and weaker with its affections and desires - All its evil passions, appetites, and inclinations."* –John Wesley

> *"And they that are Christ's - All genuine Christians have crucified the flesh - are so far from obeying its dictates and acting under its influence, that they have crucified their sensual appetites; they have nailed them to the cross of Christ, where they have expired with him; hence, says St. Paul, Romans 6:6, our old man - the*

flesh, with its affections and lusts, is crucified with him, that the body of sin might be destroyed, that henceforth we should not serve sin. By which we see that God has fully designed to save all who believe in Christ from all sin, whether outward or inward, with all the affections, irregular passions, and lusts, disorderly wishes and desires—all that a man may feel contrary to love and purity; and all that he may desire contrary to moderation and that self-denial peculiar to the Christian character." –Adam Clarke

> **"But the fruit of the Spirit is love, joy, peace, longsuffering, gentleness, goodness, faith, Meekness, temperance: against such there is no law." Galatians 5:22-23**

PRAYER: *Heavenly Father, I'd like to walk in Your bless-ed joy, filling my life to overflowing, no matter what's transpiring. LORD, I ask You to do Your deeper work in my heart, in my life. Please set apart my life to truly glorify You, being full of the fruits of Your righteousness. In Jesus' Name, amen.*

Chapter 2

God Created You to Know Him

"And this is life eternal, that they might know thee the only true God, and Jesus Christ, whom thou hast sent." John 17:3

Ask yourself, *"Do I seek to know the LORD or am I just another self-seeking Scripture skimmer who uses His Word in an attempt to use Him to get what I want?"*

Christology simply means "the study of Christ." Those who know and love Him study Him! In fact, HE is the Grand Subject of all of Holy Scripture. If we miss Him in the reading of His Word, perhaps it's due to the self-serving, self-seeking fallen nature, with no cross in our personal lives.

IF you will be planted deep into Christ, your Christology, your study of, your personal knowledge of Christ must be deep, not shallow (Colossians 2:6-10).

"And he said to them all, If any man will come after me, let him deny himself, and

take up his cross daily, and follow me. [24] For whosoever will save his life shall lose it: but whosoever will lose his life for my sake, the same shall save it." Luke 9:23-24

The only way to follow Jesus is the exact way He prescribed. **"And whosoever doth not bear his cross, and come after me, cannot be my disciple"** (Luke 14:27). To walk with Jesus, you must deny yourself and feed your spirit.

Hell is full of people who thought they were going to use Jesus to get them to Heaven but refused to seek to get to know Him on earth. Yeah, they answered His call and got saved and then fell away due to choosing to have no root in themselves—no follow through (Luke 8:11-15).

If you were saved in the past and are not presently seeking the LORD diligently, you've fallen away from Him and are in need of swift repentance before it's too late. Memorize this verse now: **"Seek the LORD and his strength, seek his face continually"** (1 Chronicles 16:11). Also, **"Seek ye the LORD while he may be found, call ye upon him while he is near"** (Isaiah 55:6).

Are You a Scripture Skimmer?

Heretics act as if they can skip over and ignore volumes of Bible verses and not have to give account to God in the end. They are self-absorbed, willingly deceived, turned over to **"strong delusion,"** and going to eternal **"damnation"** (2 Thessalonians 2:9-12).

Speaking of essential doctrine, where's the cross? Why do we nearly never hear it preached?

It would be impossible for a preacher to be taking up the cross himself and not be preaching the cross, the crucified life. What does that say for America's preachers? Read Philippians 3:18-19.

Many today skip over messages about Jesus, <u>the cross</u>, and the crucified life He commands (Luke 9:23-24). They skim Scripture in order to get to messages that feed their flesh (2 Timothy 4:2-4). There are so very many false prophets today who accommodate such. This is more than obvious in the wolves of today who are paid well for their lies while sending millions to hell.

> **"Preach the word; be instant in season, out of season; reprove, rebuke, exhort with all**

longsuffering and doctrine. [3] For the time will come when they will not endure sound doctrine; but after their own lusts shall they heap to themselves teachers, having itching ears; [4] And they shall turn away their ears from the truth, and shall be turned unto fables." 2 Timothy 4:2-4

The self-serving lightweights who many address as "pastor" don't get you into the Word for yourself because they simply want you to continue to patronize their church busine$$! Get a clue! This is completely contrary to the Holy Spirit inspired writings of Christ's apostle Paul (2 Timothy 2:15; 3:16-17; 4:2-4). ANY so-called "preacher" who won't offend you with sound doctrine filled with *all* the plain truths of Scripture is a self-serving wolf! RUN NOW!

Today's self-seeking generation has a mere outward **"form *(facade)* of godliness"** yet deny the reign of the cross of Christ in their daily lives:

"Having a form of godliness, but denying the power thereof: from such turn away. ... [7] Ever learning, and never able to come to the knowledge of the truth." 2 Timothy 3:5, 7

They have no interest in seeking and knowing Christ and therefore have no foundation in Christ and are building their house upon sinking sand. No, instead of crucifying that iniquitous nature, they look to further extend and feed it. Their **"God is their belly** *(carnal appetites)*" (Philippians 3:18-19).

In a world of religious counterfeits, who possess but a mere **"form of godliness,"** may God bless you to rise up and demonstrate true, authentic worship-filled obedience to the nail scarred risen LORD and Savior (2 Timothy 3:5). **"If the son therefore shall make you free, ye shall be free indeed"** (John 8:36).

> **"(For MANY walk, of whom I have told you often, and now tell you even weeping, that they are the enemies of the cross of Christ: 19 Whose end *is* destruction, whose God *is their* belly** *(carnal appetites)*, **and *whose* glory *is* in their shame, who mind earthly things.) 20 For our conversation** *(way of life)* **is in heaven; from whence also we look for the Saviour, the Lord Jesus Christ: 21 Who shall change our vile body, that it may be fashioned like unto his glorious body, according to the working**

whereby he is able even to subdue all things unto himself." Philippians 3:18-21

The person not crucified with Christ will communicate using only things that will bring accolades to himself. They do not want the heat, the persecutions that come with preaching the original Gospel that Jesus and His apostles preached. These are the self-serving cross-less wolves Paul warned us about specifically in Philippians 3:18-19.

Jesus warns: **"Woe unto you, when all men shall speak well of you! for so did their fathers to the false prophets"** (Luke 6:26).

Saints, Christ and His cross must be at the very center of our lives or His foundation is not being built in us and eternal ruin will be our irreversible future.

Many today, skim through Scripture to cherry pick verses for their own self-interest, staying away from certain parts of the Bible because they are too controversial—which is apostasy. The cross is not central in their lives to crucify self and so they do not seek the LORD—to love, worship, and truly know intimately.

The Pharisees, the false religionists of Christ's day did just that. They dabbled in His Word but would not submit their hearts to the LORD: **"Search the scriptures; for in them ye think ye have eternal life: and they** *(the Scriptures)* **are they which testify of me. [40] And ye will not come to me, that ye might have life"** (John 5:39-40).

> **"For ye are dead, and your life is hid with Christ in God." Colossians 3:3**

Remember the scenario Jesus foretold for many who claim Him as their **"Lord"**? Watch this:

> **"Not every one that saith unto me, Lord, Lord, shall enter into the kingdom of heaven; but he that doeth the will of my Father which is in heaven. [22] MANY will say to me in that day, Lord, Lord, have we not prophesied in thy name? and in thy name have cast out devils? and in thy name done many wonderful works? [23] And then will I profess unto them, I never knew you: depart from me, ye that work iniquity." Matthew 7:21-23**

When Jesus fed the 5,000, only 12 remained. After their carnal appetites were filled by Jesus, the 5,000 departed from Him, leaving only the twelve (John 6).

Beloved of God, getting into God's Word daily is of the utmost importance to our lives here and now... and our life in eternity. Repentance needed. Turn back to the LORD with a whole heart and seek His holy face relentlessly. Ask Him to reveal Himself, His heart in and through His Word and by His Holy Spirit (Psalms 33:11).

The LORD reveals Himself to those who diligently seek Him in His Word. **"Search the scriptures; ... they are they which testify of me"** (John 5:39).

God's Word cannot and will not get into us unless we get into it. Then, the sword of His Word will do its essential circumcising and cleansing work! **"Now ye are clean through the word which I have spoken unto you"** (John 15:3).

PRAYER: *Holy Father, please instill in me the desire to truly seek and know You from an authentically sincere and honest heart, in the fear of God. In Jesus' Name, amen.*

Chapter 3

Authentic Love

"IF ye love me, keep my commandments." John 14:15

Have you ever noticed the **"If"** of this statement by our LORD Jesus?

Okay, reread the words of Jesus above and see what comes first in the sentence— **"love,"** or keeping His commands? **"IF you love me, keep my commandments"** says Jesus (John 14:15).

IF we don't know and love Him there's no use trying to keep His Word. He's not speaking of us keeping His Word in order to earn His justification but rather as the fruit of knowing Him in a saving relationship.

> *"Few seem to understand the huge difference between obedience and legalism. We obey because we love God, and we know obedience doesn't save us. Legalism believes by obeying they are saved by it. We that are born again know that only the blood of Jesus saved us, but we also*

know that obedience proves we are saved and keeps us saved. It is joy to obey the Lord as we love what He loves and we hate what He hates. Amen." –Shirley Bruso

Enjoining Christ in love! No one of us can merit or earn His love or justification. We merely respond. YES! Obedience is extremely important but not without RELATIONSHIP.

Jesus is not glorified by the keeping of His instructions/commands by those who don't love Him. Love comes first. Loving and worshipping Him is most important to God. **"If** *(If, If)* **ye love me, keep my commandments"** (John 14:15).

Love is the governing factor: **"We love him, because he first loved us"** (1 John 4:19). Love begins with God, and any relationship requires reciprocating love—love flowing from each of the two parties.

"And Jacob served seven years for Rachel; and they seemed unto him but a few days, FOR THE LOVE HE HAD TO HER" (Genesis 29:20). Jacob didn't mind serving seven whole years for Rachel because he loved her so much. The true disciple doesn't view serving God as drudgery but rather delight because he loves God supremely!

> **"For this is the love of God, that we keep his commandments: and his commandments are not grievous." 1 John 5:3**

If we don't love Him—truly—with our whole heart, mind, and strength, He's not interested in us obeying Him (Matthew 22:37-39). Now, of course, if I truly do love Him, I *will* obey Him, and yet Jesus doesn't want us to think we are impressing Him by outward obedience only.

> **"Thou shalt love the Lord thy God…" Matthew 22:37**

> **"IF** *(If, If)* **ye love me, keep my commandments." John 14:15**

"If" denotes condition. And, if we love Jesus, obeying Him is joy, just as it was for Jacob as he served a whole seven years to obtain a lifelong marital relationship with his beloved Rachel (Genesis 29:20).

Perhaps we are not understanding the divine economy as Christ meant us to understand Him. Jesus says, **"IF you love me, keep my**

commandments" (John 15:14). It's only IF I love Jesus that He is interested in my doing the things He told His true people to do, otherwise, my good works are in vain, even if I suffer the martyrdom of my body being burned– **"And though I bestow all my goods to feed the poor, and though I give my body to be burned, and have not charity, it profiteth me nothing"** (1 Corinthians 13:2).

In the divine economy, it all begins with LOVE– **"God so LOVED the world that He gave ...."** (John 3:16). The Bible informs us that **"The Lord looketh on the heart,"** and if He sees that I don't truly love Him, He's not interested in my vain outward show (1 Samuel 16:7).

Jesus said, **"IF you love me keep my commandments"** (John 14:15), and not *"Prove you love me by keeping my commandments"* ... big difference. Jesus isn't interested in any law keeper keeping His commandments. He desires and calls His people to love Him! If not, there's no reason to try to obey Him. Such rote obedience would be a waste of time.

> **"Jesus said unto him, Thou shalt love the Lord thy God with all thy heart, and with all thy soul, and with all thy mind. 38 This is the**

first and great commandment. [39] And the second is like unto it, Thou shalt love thy neighbour as thyself. [40] On these two commandments hang all the law and the prophets." Matthew 22:37-40

Those who truly know and love Him do His commandments. They don't live on their own terms but rather on His. They delight to do His will because they truly seek, know, and love Him who bled to redeem their otherwise hopeless, wretched souls. Yet, obedience saves no one. Keeping His commandments doesn't save you. The pharisees claimed to do that while refusing to come to Christ (John 5:39-40).

No, God alone can save, and He does so on *His* terms—initial and ongoing faith **"which worketh by love"**—which is relationship. Yes, **"faith … worketh by love"** (Galatians 5:6). Remember that even if a person goes so far as to give their body to be burned and has no love (they don't love God) it's in vain! See 1 Corinthians 13:3.

1 Thessalonians 1:3 speaks to those already saved using the phrases **"work of faith and labour of love."** Please pay close attention to the words, **"faith"** and **"love."**

> **"Remembering without ceasing your work of faith, and labour of love, and patience of hope in our Lord Jesus Christ, in the sight of God and our Father;" 1 Thessalonians 1:3**

When God initially saves us, He puts a love in our hearts for Him which is manifested by putting our faith in Christ. Jesus taught that knowing the Father and Himself are cardinal in His kingdom. **"And this is life eternal** *(the whole purpose for it)*, **that they might know thee the only true God, and Jesus Christ, whom thou hast sent"** (John 17:3).

Did God send His only begotten Son to create an army of mechanical law-keepers OR a family who knows, worships, and adores Him? What does the Bible say is the cardinal reason for the whole plan of redemption? Why did God send His only begotten Son to bleed, be buried, and raised again to justify all who would come to Him? Are you familiar with what the LORD told us in Exodus 25:8; Matthew 22:37-40, and Philippians 3:10?

We must have anchored in our hearts this glorious truth of knowing Him! Nothing else matters if we don't relish Him, adore Him, and worship Him. If you name the name of Jesus Christ, it will greatly benefit your life, understanding, and ministry to memorize the words of the very Redeemer Himself as recorded in John 17:3. More on that later.

If we love the LORD and our neighbor truly, we will not steal, lie, covet, bear false witness, hate, commit adultery, or any other sins but will be walking in God's perfect will. It's really quite simple actually. But first we must examine this day if we truly love Him.

Travis Bryan III writes:

> *"Holiness is first and foremost agape love. Unconditional love for all, including enemies of us and enemies of God. The over-emphasis on repentance can make us the initiator and God the responder if we are not careful. God is always the initiator."*

It is my opinion that we should be very careful not to over-emphasize obedience while neglecting to preach and live out the command to know, love, and abide in Christ. All of our outward obedience is in vain if we don't authentically love him. A number of preachers seem to be doing this and are calling countless people to worship at the altar of self by perpetrating the false notion that Christ's one perfect sacrifice was not enough. This seems to resonate in the hearts of those who are not truly and unreservedly surrendered to Christ and who want to feel as if they are helping to earn their own salvation which is impossible. What does Romans 4:4-5 tell us?

So, while it is absolute that ALL who have saving faith in Christ are obedient and have good fruit in their lives, those good works and good fruit aren't what saves them. No, good fruit merely gives evidence that there is a relationship. Christ alone can save, and He does that instantly when a lost soul believes upon Him (John 6:47; Acts 16:31; Romans 5:1, etc.).

The Great Shepherd of His sheep keeps His people saved as they keep themselves in the love of God, **"looking for the mercy of our Lord Jesus Christ unto eternal life"** (Jude 21: 1 Peter 1:5).

> **"Keep yourselves in the love of God, looking for the mercy of our Lord Jesus Christ unto eternal life." Jude 21**

The story of Jesus, Mary, and Martha is yet another place in the Scriptures of truth that clearly reveals what God is looking for from us—to love and to worship Him supremely.

> **"Now it came to pass, as they went, that he entered into a certain village: and a certain woman named Martha received him into her house. 39 And she had a sister called Mary, which also sat at Jesus' feet, and heard his word. 40 But Martha was cumbered about much serving, and came to him, and said, Lord, dost thou not care that my sister hath left me to serve alone? bid her therefore that she help me. 41 And Jesus answered and said unto her, Martha, Martha, thou art careful and troubled about many things: 42 But one thing is needful: and Mary hath chosen that good part, which shall not be taken away from her." Luke 10:38-42**

Jesus speaks to us of an abiding union/relationship with Him where He calls us His friends. I want to encourage you to read John 15 closely this week. In this discourse on the Husbandman (the Father), the Vine (Jesus), and the branches (us), you will note that the relationship precedes the fruit bearing. While the fruit *reveals* the root, as testimony of the relationship, fruit doesn't save, neither does obedience.

God does require us to obey Him by putting our faith in Christ to save us. It is He alone who saves us. Ephesians 2:8-10 reveals that we are saved by His grace through our faith and that we are **"his workmanship, created in Christ Jesus unto good works."**

Consider that our LORD was **"moved with compassion"** toward those in need (Matthew 9:36). The great apostle said: **"the love of Christ constraineth** *(compels)* **us"** (2 Corinthians 5:14).

At times we quote 1 John 2:4 and yet, let's look at a wider angle of this passage:

> **"And hereby we do know that we know him, if we keep his commandments. [4] He that saith, I know him, and keepeth not his commandments, is a liar, and the truth is not in him. [5] But whoso keepeth his word, in him verily is the love of God perfected: hereby know we that we are in him. [6] He that saith he abideth in him ought himself also so to walk, even as he walked." 1 John 2:3-6**

"But go ye and learn what that meaneth, I will have mercy, and not sacrifice..." Matthew 9:13

"And rend your heart, and not your garments, and turn unto the Lord your God: for he is gracious and merciful, slow to anger, and of great kindness, and repenteth him of the evil." Joel 2:13

Is loving God more important that obeying God? Both are obviously important and yet, in the divine economy, which is most important?

"Jesus said unto him, Thou shalt love the Lord thy God with all thy heart, and with all thy soul, and with all thy mind. 38 This is the first and great commandment. 39 And the second is like unto it, Thou shalt love thy neighbour as thyself. 40 On these two commandments hang all the law and the prophets." Matthew 22:37-40

Am I choosing and learning to **"love the Lord"** with my whole heart?

Andre Alexis writes:

"Christianity is more than merely believing and obeying commands and reaping the promises of God. Christianity is not a religion: it is a relationship. And a relationship requires communication. Therefore, prayer is essential, because it is through prayer that you and I communicate with our heavenly Father."

This is a simple truth and yet bears stating as brother Andre did above. This is especially important due to the epidemic of charlatans which have promulgated a "what's-in-it-for-me" self-serving lifestyle upon millions who don't bother to truly lay down their lives and see with their own eyes the full counsel of our LORD's Word which actually communicates the very **"thoughts of his heart"** (Psalms 33:11).

The LORD wants a relationship with each of His children. He's not just there to answer our every prayer while we commit spiritual adultery by wasting our time/lives in this fleeting world playing games, giving hours to frivolous foolishness, etc. No, He wants our hearts.

Jesus told us in John 17:3 the reason the Father sent Him. This was David's and Paul's whole goal in their respective earthly lives (Psalms 27:4, 8;

Philippians 3:10). Jesus told us He wants an abiding relationship that bears fruit that remains, to His eternal glory (John 15:1-16).

After being saved, under the New Covenant, it's not law keeping but rather abiding in Christ, amen? John 15: **"Abide in me."**

An abiding relationship with Jesus will always bear the fruit of authenticity. **"My little children, let us not love in word, neither in tongue; but in deed and in truth"** (1 John 3:18).

Love is the cardinal evidence or fruit that one knows God. **"Herein is my Father glorified, that ye bear much fruit; so shall ye be my disciples." John 15:8**

Do we truly know Him who **"is love"**? See 1 John 4:8, 16. Love is a divine attribute that is, without exception, resident in every man who is truly in right standing with God (Galatians 5:22-23).

PRAYER: *Heavenly Father, I come to You impoverished in spirit. For without You dear LORD, we can do nothing. You are love and I am not and yet, I ask You here and now to more deeply imbue my innermost man with and teach me Your love. In the name of Jesus Christ. Amen.*

Chapter 4

Authentic Fellowship

**"And they continued stedfastly in the
apostles' doctrine and fellowship, and in
breaking of bread, and in prayers. 43 And fear
came upon every soul: and many wonders and
signs were done by the apostles. 44 And all that
believed were together, and had all things
common; 45 And sold their possessions and
goods, and parted them to all men, as every
man had need. 46 And they, continuing daily
with one accord in the temple, and breaking
bread from house to house, did eat their meat
with gladness and singleness of heart,
47 Praising God, and having favour with all the
people. And the Lord added to the church
daily such as should be saved." Acts 2:42-47**

True New Testament fellowship—oh so simple, so uncluttered, unencumbered!

Notice in Acts 2:42, the four simple elements that made up the fellowship of the earliest followers of Jesus, in which they "**continued stedfastly**":

- **"the apostles' doctrine"**

- **"fellowship"**
- **"breaking of bread"**
- **"prayers"**

"And they, continuing daily with one accord in the temple, and breaking bread from house to house, did eat their meat with gladness and singleness of heart." Acts 2:46

The word "weekly" appears 0 (zero) times in the Bible. The word **"daily"** appears 63 times in God's Word. Notice they went **"from house to house,"** and there were no official church buildings yet where in most cases mere men rule.

Authentic worship to the LORD is *daily*, not weekly, and among the people of God is the exhortation to daily remain free from all sin (Matthew 6:11) to be ready for our LORD's soon return! **"But exhort one another daily, while it is called To day; lest any of you be hardened through the deceitfulness of sin"** (Hebrews 3:13).

"Not forsaking the assembling of ourselves together, as the manner of some is; but exhorting one another: and so much the

more, as ye see the day approaching." Hebrews 10:25

Keeping Things Super Simple

Keep it biblical, right? Here is a Bible study format for two or more: Each person involved in the group individually is given a Bible verse or passage and studies that text to be examined when the gathering takes place. They simply share what they are learning about that portion of Scripture and the others chime in. The best way to LEARN is to TEACH (Acts 2:42; Colossians 3:16; 1 Timothy 4:6; 2 Timothy 3:16-17; Revelation 1:3, etc.).

"Admonish One Another"

Jesus, **"that Great Shepherd of the sheep,"** gives the regular, perpetual call to be **"ready,"** hence the instruction to exhort and to **"admonish one another."**

"... admonish one another." Romans 15:14

"For ye were as sheep going astray; but are now returned unto the Shepherd and Bishop of your souls." 1 Peter 2:25

Amidst the earliest followers of Jesus Christ, who continued steadfastly in the apostle's doctrine, fellowship, breaking of bread, and prayers, one can ascertain that godly admonishment was a regular part of their fellowship.

Fellowship involves interacting in relationship with the members of Christ's body. Three chapters which contain such rich content concerning the body of Christ would be Romans 12, 1 Corinthians 12, and Ephesians 4. May you be encouraged to prayerfully pour over these beautiful chapters in God's Word.

Yes, our LORD and Savior is the **"Shepherd and Bishop"** over the souls of His beloved people, and admonishments would be one element of true fellowship. Let's take a look.

What Does it Mean to Exhort and "Admonish" Someone?

The words **"exhort"** and **"exhorting"** appear 20 times in the New Testament canon.

"To ***'exhort'*** *– Gk. parakaleō - to call near, that is, invite, invoke (by imploration, exhortation or consolation): - beseech, call for, (be of good)*

comfort, desire, (give) exhort(ation), intreat, pray.

The words **"admonish,"** or **"admonishing"** appear four times in the New Testament Scriptures. The biblical instruction to **"admonish"** means *"to put in mind, to caution, reprove gently, to warn."*

"Let the word of Christ dwell in you richly in all wisdom; teaching and <u>admonishing one another</u> in psalms and hymns and spiritual songs, singing with grace in your hearts to the Lord. [17] And whatsoever ye do in word or deed, do all in the name of the Lord Jesus, giving thanks to God and the Father by him." Colossians 3:16-17

As the Word of God dwells richly, abundantly in our midst, so shall the admonishments of the LORD take their place in and among us. Admonishing and encouraging other believers as we share in the Word of God, learning and living it, glorifies the LORD. Godly admonishment will always come out of the Word of God, in the love and wisdom of God, through crucified vessels. It will always be the Word of God and not the selfish whims of mere men.

"Behave Yourself"

Years ago, a dear brother in Christ I knew used to tell the brothers around him, including myself, to *"Behave yourself."* He did this as he looked you straight in the eyes and his tone completely lacked self-righteousness, and was instead, loving, firm. In his exhortation he was caring, yet resolute, and that godly tone carried through in his words and were nearly as important as these words of exhortation he would lovingly charge other brothers with.

> **"And I myself also am persuaded of you, my brethren, that ye also are full of goodness, filled with all knowledge, able also to <u>admonish one another</u>." Romans 15:14**

The apostle was persuaded that the brethren of Christ at the church, the body of Christ in Rome, Italy were...

- **"full of goodness,"**
- **"filled with all knowledge,"**
- **"able also to <u>admonish one another</u>"**

Notice the absence of personal pride in the brethren at Rome. It takes authentic humility and oneness with God in Christ to fill a man's heart with His **"goodness"** (John 15, 17). It takes a whole Bible to make a whole disciple and when we are **"filled with all knowledge"** of God's Word, we shall be **"able also to admonish one another"** (Romans 15:14).

Adam Clarke on Romans 15:14:

"They were so full of goodness and love. Filled with all knowledge – So completely instructed in the mind and design of God, relative to their calling, and the fruit which they were to bring forth to the glory of God, that they were well-qualified to give one another suitable exhortations on every important point. If they were all filled with knowledge, there was little occasion for them to admonish one another; but by this they were well-qualified to admonish others – to impart the wisdom they had to those who were less instructed."

Beloved saint of Christ, do you realize the divine blessing that will come upon your life as you ask the Father to break you and fill you full of His love? Read 1 Corinthians 13 daily in the morning this week and memorize John 13:35. **"That Christ may dwell in your hearts by faith; that ye, being rooted and grounded in love"** (Ephesians 3:17).

As usual, among the saints of Christ, in oneness with Christ and the Father, being crucified with Christ, and empowered by the Holy Spirit, love must be the driving motive. We must be moved with God's love as it permeates our inner man.

> **"That their hearts might be comforted, being knit together in love, and unto all riches of the full assurance of understanding, to the acknowledgement of the mystery of God, and of the Father, and of Christ; [3] In whom are hid all the treasures of wisdom and knowledge." Colossians 2:2-3**

As we are truly crucified with Christ, we shall walk in the mind of Christ, and all things shall be done in His love for the blessing, the betterment of others whom we will **"esteem ... other better than"** ourselves (Philippians 2:3-5; John 15, 17).

KJV Webster's 1828 Dictionary Definition:

"ADMON'ISH, v.t. L. *admoneo, ad and moneo,* to teach, warn, admonish.

1. "To warn or notify of a fault; to reprove with mildness. Count him not as an enemy but admonish him as a brother. 2 Thessalonians 3.

2. "To counsel against wrong practices; to caution or advise. Admonish one another in psalms and hymns. Colossians 3.

3. "To instruct or direct. Moses was admonished of God when he was about to make the tabernacle. Hebrews 8.

4. "In ecclesiastical affairs, to reprove a member of the church for a fault, either publicly or privately; the first step of church discipline. It is followed by of, or against; as, to admonish of a fault committed, or against committing a fault. It has a like use in colleges."

"And we beseech you, brethren, to know them which labour among you, and are over you in the Lord, and <u>admonish you</u>;" 1 Thessalonians 5:12

"Yet count him not as an enemy, but <u>admonish him as a brother</u>." 2 Thessalonians 3:15

Another rendering of the biblical word and instruction to **"admonish"**....

"Transitive verb. 1a: to indicate duties or obligations to. b: to express warning or disapproval to especially in a gentle, earnest, or solicitous manner (were ***admonished*** *for being late). 2: to give friendly earnest advice or encouragement to* ***admonish*** *them to be careful."*

Provoking One Another unto Love and Good Works

"And having an high priest over the house of God; [22] Let us draw near with a true heart in full assurance of faith, having our hearts sprinkled from an evil conscience, and our bodies washed with pure water. [23] Let us hold fast the profession of our faith without wavering; (for he is faithful that promised;) [24] And <u>let us consider one another to provoke unto love and to good works</u>: [25] Not forsaking the assembling of

ourselves together, as the manner of some is; but exhorting one another: and so much the more, as ye see the day approaching." Hebrews 10:22-25

May the LORD bless us with admonishment for His glory, empowered by His Holy Spirit and love.

May God bless us to be rooted in Christ our LORD, one with Him and bearing His fruit—the fruit that He alone can produce in this relationship (John 15, 17). Do we readily own the divine themes of John 17 and then 15? Life changer! Gain the vision of this divine masterpiece and work from this biblical grid beloved!

In John 17, Jesus prays to the Father to make us one with them, and then in John 15 our LORD speaks of that abiding relationship for which He saved us, and the corresponding fruit produced by God for His glory! May it be. Let it be in each of our lives this day and this week dear LORD Jesus!

As we allow "**Jesus, the Great Shepherd of the sheep**" to guide our lives, through our daily cross relationship, He will lead us beside the still waters into fruitful pastures that glorify His holy Name (John 10; Psalms 23).

PRAYER: *Heavenly Father, thank You for finding and saving Your beloved people by the blood of Your only begotten Son. We love You dear Father and LORD Jesus Christ! Make us to be one with You and therefore to bear the fruit that glorifies Your holy Name. I am no longer my own but Yours, bought by Your precious blood and now abandoned to Your perfect will, leading, guidance and truth. Please allow Your command to "admonish one another" be found throughout Your body as it pleases You. In the name of Jesus Christ, amen!*

Chapter 5

Authentic Humility

"Pride goeth before destruction, and an haughty spirit before a fall." Proverbs 16:18

What goes before **"destruction"** and a **"fall"**? **"Pride,"** right?

Pride is exactly what happened to Saul and happens to so many today. When men experience some measure of victory, they are then prone to pride instead of thanksgiving . . . not humility and the cross.

> **"Then Samuel said unto Saul, Stay, and I will tell thee what the LORD hath said to me this night. And he said unto him, Say on. [17] And Samuel said, WHEN THOU WAS LITTLE IN THINE OWN SIGHT, wast thou not made the head of the tribes of Israel, and the LORD anointed thee king over Israel?" 1 Samuel 15:16-17**

As we serve the LORD and He uses us, we must be careful to never think of ourselves beyond being blessed to be the children of God, having our names written in His book of life (Luke 10:20). **"Wherefore let him that thinketh he standeth take heed lest he fall"** (1 Corinthians 10:12).

Genuine Humility vs. the Sin of Pride

> **"Only by pride cometh contention: but with the well advised is wisdom." Proverbs 13:10**

"Only by pride" comes contention, comes discord between man and man and between God and man. Pride precedes man's destruction and simply cannot be allowed in our lives if we intend to be with Jesus now and forever. The last time pride was found in Heaven, God violently ejected it!

The middle letter of each of these biblical words below is, you guessed it - I.

Pr-i-de
vs.
Cruc-i-fied

Those not living the crucified life are walking in pride, full of pride—without exception—and will be **"destroyed." "He, that being often reproved hardeneth his neck** *(pride)*, **shall**

suddenly be destroyed, and that without remedy" (Proverbs 29:1).

Without Jesus today, without my abiding in/with Him, I can do nothing and bring forth no fruit to please Him (John 15:5). To abide in Jesus is to abide with absolute humility, crying out to the LORD that He **"must increase, but I must decrease"** (John 3:30).

The cross reveals your sin, and God's love, not how wonderful you are! Repent!

The cross of Jesus Christ is not about how wonderful we are but rather how wicked and sinful we are and how loving God is to have sent His only begotten Son to die on Calvary's cross for our sins to bring us back to Him, **"while we were yet sinners"** (John 3:16; Romans 5:6, 8). Get on your face before God and give Him thanks and glory for finding and saving your wretched soul and for His unfathomable, **"unspeakable gift"** of Jesus! See 2 Corinthians 9:15.

Armed and Dangerous!

Are we armed with humility? The one who authentically possesses the posture of a pure humble heart is the one God is going use, bless, and bring into eternal glory. **"Blessed are the poor in spirit: for theirs is the kingdom of heaven"** (Matthew 5:3). **"Blessed are the pure in heart: for they shall see God"** (Matthew 5:8).

Lots of Americans who believe in the Second Amendment of the Constitution of the United States are armed and ready physically, yet only a few are armed and dangerous spiritually. Which one of these **"armed"** positions will the LORD reward? The answer is obvious. **"We wrestle not against flesh and blood ..."** (Ephesians 6:12). Are you armed with weapons for self-protection and yet not armed in the Spirit with the armor of God? (Ephesians 6:10-18)

The cross of Christ, applied to our personal life, conquers all sin. This is key because sin gives place to Satan (James 4:7). May God bless each of us, His children, to begin to grasp and experience the divine concept and working of His cross—to understand that Jesus died once to conquer all sin on that tree upon which He bled. He also sent us forth to be crucified **"WITH"** Him so that all sin is conquered and overcome in our daily lives (Romans 6; Galatians 2:20). **"Arm yourselves"**!

"Forasmuch then as Christ hath suffered for us in the flesh, arm yourselves likewise with the same mind: for he that hath suffered in the flesh hath ceased from sin;" 1 Peter 4:1

All hell broke loose on Satan when Jesus was raised from the dead—and all hell breaks loose daily on the powers and works of darkness when the crucified saints are walking in resurrection power! See Romans 8:11; 1 Corinthians 2:8; 2 Corinthians 4:10-12 and Colossians 2:14-17.

This is the ultimate use of the phrase "armed and dangerous"! When we are armed with, partaking of that bless-ed cross, crucified life, there will be that dangerous-to-the-devil resurrection power of Jesus Christ bursting forth in our lives.

In responding to an emailed question, the following reply was given:

"Yes, we are saved by grace through faith in the finished work of Christ and that's initial salvation. In teaching us how to walk with Him, (continuing to abide and remain in Him), Christ and His apostles taught the need to live the crucified life, the daily cross (Luke 9:23-24;

Romans 6; 2 Corinthians 4:10-12; Colossians 3:3; Galatians 2:20, etc.)"

Our obedience to God is not *earning* our salvation thereafter yet is rather out of our love for Him, and yet there's our flesh that would destroy our relationship with Him who is **"Holy, holy, holy"** unless the cross separated sin and Satan from us (Isaiah 6:3; Revelation 4:8). **"He that is dead is freed from sin"** and yet otherwise, **"The wages of sin is death** *(separation from God)"* (Romans 6:7, 23).

Our walk with the LORD is a test of our love for Him, or lack thereof (Matthew 22:37-39). **"No man can serve two masters"** (Matthew 6:24). Will I love Him more than self–with the defiling, separating sin that self wants to perform? Read Romans 6 and 7.

There are two parts of the cross–the atoning death Jesus alone accomplished on the cross– **"It is finished,"** and the cross He commanded us to take up daily as we are **"crucified WITH"** Him.

In this second part of the cross, we have died to our old nature and buried it so that we can partake of Christ's divine nature, as He raises us upward in His grace and power into full victory and fruitfulness in pleasing Him. His divine power which works in us keeps us from the things that displease Him, which He calls sin (John 19:30; Romans 6-8; Galatians 2:20; 5:16-24; Philippians 2:13; 2 Peter 1:3-8). May the blessed cross, the death and burial become a reality in each of our daily lives that Christ might perpetually raise us upward in His power (Romans 8:11; 2 Corinthians 4:10-12).

The LORD who saved us by His grace and perfect sacrifice also instructed us on how to follow and to remain in Him—to **"abide"** (John 15). The cross is the divine prescription for remaining, for continuing in Him and enduring to the end to be with Him eternally in glory! See Luke 9:23-24.

Possessing an Authentic "Less than the Least" Disposition

"Unto me, who am less than the least of all saints, is this grace given, that I should preach among the Gentiles the unsearchable riches of Christ;" Ephesians 3:8

We should see ourselves as the most undeserving of the saving grace of Christ. We should say before our God, with the man who hung his head low as he prayed and said, **"God be merciful to me a sinner"** (Luke 18:13).

God calls those whom He saves to relish the great love, forgiveness, grace, and mercy He has shown upon us **"WHILE we were yet sinners"** (Romans 5:6-8). This is the disposition of the true disciple. In fact, He calls us to lift up and prefer others ABOVE ourselves.

> **"Let nothing be done through strife or vainglory; but in lowliness of mind let each esteem other better than themselves. 4 Look not every man on his own things, but every man also on the things of others. 5 Let this mind be in you, which was also in Christ Jesus:" Philippians 2:3-5**

The above passage is a great way to begin our day, every morning.

Those who truly seek and love the LORD, love also all men. Having freely received it, they desire to pour out the message of Christ's saving mercy on others.

Memorize the words of our LORD recorded in Matthew 22:37-40.

> **"Whosoever believeth that Jesus is the Christ is born of God: and every one that loveth him that begat loveth him also that is begotten of him." 1 John 5:1**

Those who are **"born of God"** love all others who are His with a special kingdom familial love.

As end time events unfold before our very eyes, the heart cry of the sincere disciple is to be authentic with God and man. The shape of the cross: The cross beam first goes *upward*, then *outward*. The life of Christ's disciple is to be lived *upward* to God and *outward* to others. Loving God *vertically* enables us to love others—for His love to pour through us *horizontally*. As we are loving God truly, we are seeking the LORD above continually, and He is dispensing His grace and love into us and outward to love others.

> **"Jesus said unto him, Thou shalt love the Lord thy God with all thy heart, and with all thy soul, and with all thy mind. 38 This is the first and great commandment. 39 And the second is like unto it, Thou shalt love thy neighbour as thyself. 40 On these two**

commandments hang all the law and the prophets." Matthew 22:37-40

This life as Christ's **"ambassadors"** is all about loving the LORD supremely and thereafter loving all men, all others, above ourselves (2 Corinthians 5:17-20; Philippians 2:3-5).

World: "Follow your heart."
Jesus: "Follow me."

World: "Believe in yourself."
Jesus "Believe in me.

World: "Discover yourself."
Jesus: "Deny yourself."

World: "Be true to you."
Jesus: "Be true to me."

The true disciple sees himself as absolutely undeserving of and infinitely blessed to have been found and saved by the LORD Jesus Christ! He sees himself like Paul– **"LESS than the least of all saints"** (Ephesians 3:8).

"The Lord's mandate for humility is a powerful truth that seems so small to most...but what God

requires is our hearts to become as little children, humble before our Abba Father. Like the apostle Paul said: 'I count all things ... but dung, that I may win Christ.' Anything and everything falls short of knowing Jesus Christ. He is our everything." –Nancy Cote

The apostle Paul had his personal testimony of being saved by the grace of Christ and considered himself to be, not the least, but rather **"LESS than the least"** of all saints in Christ. In my opinion, this should be the only thing you and I should disagree with Paul concerning. Paul didn't know us when he said that, right? ;) Get the point? You and I, as we see the truth about our own utter iniquitous depravity (Romans 7), should view ourselves as **"LESS than the least of all saints"** (Ephesians 3:8). We should also agree with the divine truth uttered from the great apostle of Christ and recorded below:

> **"For I know that in me (that is, in my flesh,) dwelleth <u>no good thing</u>: for to will is present with me; but how to perform that which is good I find not." Romans 7:18**

Defusing the iniquity of self-righteousness increases exponentially when we begin learning the biblical doctrine of fallen mankind – which slays each of us to the ground in one swipe of the divine pen (Genesis 6:5, 12; Jeremiah 17:9; Romans 7:18; Psalms 39:4-5).

"The best of men are but men at the best." –F.B. Meyer

"LORD, make me to know mine end, and measure of my days, what it is; that I may know how frail I am. [5] Behold, thou hast made my days as an handbreadth; and mine age is as nothing before thee: verily every man at his best state is altogether vanity. Selah." Psalms 39:4-5

How Do You See Yourself?

Some among us recklessly pretend to be sinless. This seems apparent in the way they harshly, mercilessly judge others. Yet, God's Word warns each of us: **"Be sure your sin will find you out"** (Numbers 32:23).

Instead of covering our sins, denying we've committed them, we must walk in transparency with our LORD and simply admit them honestly and forsake them:

"He that covereth his sins shall not prosper: but whoso confesseth and forsaketh them shall have mercy." Proverbs 28:13

"If we say that we have no sin, we deceive ourselves, and the truth is not in us. [9] If we confess our sins, he is faithful and just to forgive us our sins, and to cleanse us from all unrighteousness. [10] If we say that we have not sinned, we make him a liar, and his word is not in us." 1 John 1:8-10

We must view all things from God's perspective, through the eyes of Holy Scripture, lest we be deceived.

ALL sin is known to God (Proverbs 15:3). He knows every sin we've ever committed. Just because we didn't always get caught by mere men, just because men didn't know, doesn't negate this fact.

"Some men's sins are open beforehand *(public, known to men)*, **going before to judgment; and some men they follow after** *(unknown to men)*." **1 Timothy 5:24**

Some men's sins are public while others are hidden for now and yet God sees and will bring them all to the light after death. Nothing is hidden from His eyes (Proverbs 15:3; Hebrews 4:13).

In order to see the person most in need of divine mercy ... just look in the mirror. The sin that should concern us the most is our own.

Mercy! Back up the dump truck and unload it on others AS WE OURSELVES DESPERATELY need it from God! He requires this authenticity! Hell is full of self-righteous, merciless religious hypocrites. Jesus says the harlots will be in Heaven before they will!

> **"Jesus saith unto them, Verily I say unto you, That the publicans and the harlots go into the kingdom of God before you." Matthew 21:31**

One commentary on this passage states:

"Christ forces from the unwilling hearers an answer which, at the moment, they do not see will condemn themselves. Unaccustomed to be criticized and put to the question, wrapped in a self-complacent righteousness, which was generally undisturbed, they missed the bearing of

the parable on their own case, and answered without hesitation, as any unprejudiced person would have decided. The first; i.e. the son who first refused, but afterwards repented and went. Verily I say unto you. Jesus drives the moral home to the hearts of these hypocrites. The publicans and the harlots. He specifies these excommunicated sinners as examples of those represented by the first son. Go into the kingdom of God before you; προαὶγουσιν ὑμας: are preceding you. This was the fact which Jesus saw and declared, he does not cut off all hope that the Pharisees might follow, if they willed to do so; he only shows that they have lost the position which they ought to have occupied, and that those whom they despised and spurned have accepted the offered salvation and shall have their reward. We must remark that the Lord has no censure for those who sometime were disobedient, but afterwards repented; his rebuke falls on the professors and self-righteous, who ought to have been leaders and guides, and were in truth impious and irreligious." –Pulpit Commentary

In this statement and much more of what we see in the Word, it seems to reveal that God expresses to us that the vilest of sinners, are the self-righteous religionists.

"As far as the east is from the west, so far hath he removed our transgressions from us." Psalms 103:12

Think of the worst sin you have ever committed: Now, if we want all our sins removed **"as far as the east is from the west,"** God requires that we **"fear him"** and therefore obey Him by forgiving others who have wronged us. All who fear God obey God and show His mercy and love to others, as they've received (Matthew 10:8). The preceding words to the verse above (Psalms 103:12), contain the divinely-opposed condition— **"so great is his mercy toward them that fear him"** (Psalms 103:11). Fearing God is an essential. Dare we never miss the conditions for God's blessings.

May the LORD bless us to be ridded of any self-righteous attitudes and words of condemnation toward others and relish His mercy that we never deserved but that God provided through the blood of the cross of His only begotten Son. May we release forever the hand of judgment from around the necks of others (Matthew 18:21-35).

Saved by Divine Mercy

"Not by works of righteousness which we have done, but according to his mercy he saved us, by the washing of regeneration, and renewing of the Holy Ghost; 6 Which he shed on us abundantly through Jesus Christ our Saviour; 7 That being justified by his grace, we should be made heirs according to the hope of eternal life." Titus 3:5-7

Do we still think we were worthy in ourselves to be forgiven, saved? Not! God did it out of His sheer love! Can we examine that idea?

"But we are all as an unclean thing, and all our righteousnesses are as filthy rags..." Isaiah 64:6

"As it is written, There is none righteous, no, not one:" Romans 3:10

"I am not worthy of the least of all the mercies, and of all the truth, which thou hast shewed unto thy servant." Genesis 32:10

PRAYER: *Precious holy Father, thank You for loving us and sending Your only begotten Son to die for our sins while we were still in sin. Please reduce me and vanquish the foolish, unwarranted pride of my heart and life. It's not by any works of righteousness which I have done but rather according to Your sheer mercy and love that You sent Your only begotten Son to die for me. Please wash away all my sins afresh in the blood of Jesus dear Father. May my heart be ever and always grateful for Your matchless Son and salvation. I love You Father. I love You Jesus. In the name of Jesus, amen.*

Chapter 6

My Foolishness and Sins

"O God, thou knowest my foolishness; and MY SINS are not hid from thee." Psalms 69:5

Like the psalmist, isn't it just better to admit when we are wrong, to openly admit we are not sinless perfection but rather utterly, perpetually in need of God's grace?

Sin by any other name is still sin:

It is not an affair, it is adultery.

It is not premarital sex, it is fornication.

It is not homosexuality, it is sodomy.

It is not an obsession, it is idolatry.

It is not fibbing, it is lying.

It is not an abortion, it is murder.

Don't whitewash sin, repent of it!

God knew the foolishness and wickedness of David's heart and the hearts of all men (Jeremiah 17:9).

"Foolishness" is one of the sins Jesus cites as coming from corrupted hearts and is the opposite of authentic, honest worship. Anyone else realize how foolish they can be?

> **"For from within, out of the heart men, proceed evil thoughts, adulteries, fornications, murders, 22 Thefts, covetousness wickedness, deceit, lasciviousness, an evil eye, blasphemy, pride, foolishness: 23 All these evil things come from within, and defile the man." Mark 7:21-23**

David spoke of **"my sins"** which means he took personal responsibility for his sin instead of covering or making excuse for his sins. The sweet Psalmist of Israel declared his sins, denounced, and confessed them to the LORD (Psalms 69:5).

God can and will work with the honest. He requires honesty for glory (Proverbs 28:13; Luke 8:15).

The LORD knows the wickedness of our hearts. If I choose not to be truly **"crucified with**

Christ" and therefore dwell on wickedness of any kind, He sees all the thoughts that I allow to occupy my mind that are not holy, but sinful— **"evil concupiscence"** (Colossians 3:5).

He sees where the enemy or my own un-mortified sinful nature feeds and allows wicked thoughts into my mind. Have you ever not guarded your heart by casting down wicked imaginations? (2 Corinthians 10:5; Proverbs 4:23) Can you relate? Yet, this must not be (Romans 8:5-8; 12:1-2; Ephesians 4:22-24).

> **"Mortify therefore your members which are upon the earth; fornication, uncleanness, inordinate affection, evil concupiscence** *(secret desire for that which is forbidden by God)*, **and covetousness, which is idolatry:" Colossians 3:5**

> **"For to be carnally minded is death; but to be spiritually minded is life and peace." Romans 8:6**

Those who walk with the LORD, who is the **"Prince of peace,"** walk in purity of heart and are possessed with **"the peace of God, which passeth all understanding"** (Isaiah 9:6-7; Philippians 4:7).

> *"If God be our God, He will give us peace in trouble. When there is a storm without, He will make peace within. The world can create trouble in peace, but God can create peace in trouble."* –Thomas Watson

The cross, purity of heart, and the peace of God go hand in hand. They are inseparable.

Did I mention Matthew 5:8? Have you memorized the words of our LORD recorded here? **"Blessed are the pure in heart: for they shall see God"** (Matthew 5:8).

Without the present working of Christ in our lives, the thoughts of our hearts are **"only evil continually"** (Genesis 6:5).

It would be deceitful, self-deception on our part to believe we are going to **"see God"**–to walk with Him now and eternally be with God without a purified heart, cleansed by the working of the LORD in our submitted lives. Who did Jesus tell us is going to **"see God"**? **"Blessed are the pure in heart: for they shall see God"** (Matthew 5:8).

Every single day presents the opportunity to overcome, yet this can only happen as we choose to do things God's way—the cross (Romans 6-8; Job 9:20; Proverbs 20:9; Galatians 2:20). The cross, the crucified life, is the divine answer to an impure heart and life. Though many who claim to belong to Christ believe that they have no personal responsibility in their salvation, the Bible reveals the contrary.

> **"Wherefore, my beloved, as ye have always obeyed, not as in my presence only, but now much more in my absence, work out your own salvation with fear and trembling. 13 For it is God which worketh in you both to will and to do of his good pleasure." Philippians 2:12-13**

God doesn't separate our current spiritual state from what we think/meditate upon. Scary, huh? **"For as he thinketh in his heart, so *is* he"** (Proverbs 23:7). He knows our thoughts and we choose our thoughts.

We can hide our true spiritual state from men but not the Almighty. We can smile and seem to be rejoicing and even ministering in the love of the LORD, and at the same time, allow iniquities to make a nest in our hearts and minds. The big question is: What am I entertaining in the theatre of my mind and heart? And am I in need of true repentance and a time of fasting and prayer for cleansing? See Joel 2:12.

"If I regard iniquity in my heart, the Lord will not hear me" (Psalms 66:18). The Hebrew word for **"regard"** is *raah,* and its definition as used here, is to: *"presently approve, consider, enjoy, experience, gaze upon in one's heart."*

I am not a good person. Neither are you. **"There is none righteous, no, not one"** (Romans 3:10). Admit it. The Bible and our own failing experience in this life clearly reveal such to be the case. The sooner we become HONEST with that which is more than obvious, announcing freely and transparently that there is **"no good thing"** in us except CHRIST, the sooner God will begin a fresh, deeper work in us! See Romans 7:18, 24—the cross!

> **"For I know that in me (that is, in my flesh,) dwelleth no good thing: for to will is present with me; but how to perform that which is good I find not." Romans 7:18**

Until you realize the depth of your depravity, you are not going to realize or understand the purpose of the cross Jesus ordained for your daily life (Luke 9:23-24). He desires to be at the center of your daily life and that requires you getting out of the way. The cross crucifies us out of His way!

Yet instead of taking personal responsibility to be crucified with Christ, the evil nature wants to nit-pick, to be a busybody about the sins of others. According to the Son of God, the definition of a **"hypocrite"** is one who stands in judgment of others while he himself has sin in his own life that he hasn't dealt with in repentance before a holy God (Matthew 7:1-5). Such a man is heaping undiluted judgment **"down upon his own pate** *(head)*" (Psalms 7:16).

> **"For he shall have judgment without mercy, that hath shewed no mercy; and mercy rejoiceth against judgment." James 2:13**

If you've confessed and forsaken your past sins, they do not disqualify you from serving God and preaching Christ's Gospel! No, ... preach! See Philippians 3:13-14; 1 John 1:9.

Backsliding Begins in the Heart

"The <u>backslider in heart</u> shall be filled with his own ways: and a good man shall be satisfied from himself." Proverbs 14:14

The **"backslider in heart"** is one whose heart affections are not presently fixed upon the LORD and His kingdom. Usually, the backslider does not know he is slidden back. He has allowed his heart to wander by not taking his thoughts captive and has become deceived thereby. The **"cares of this world, and the deceitfulness of riches, and the lusts of other things"** have entered in to **"choke the word"** because he has not tilled (cultivated) the soil of his heart through regular communion with the Savior along with obeying Him in the denial of the self-life (John 3:30; Luke 9:23-26).

Take notice in Proverbs 14:14 that backsliding is a matter of the heart. **"The backslider <u>in heart</u> shall be filled with his own ways: and a good man shall be satisfied from himself"** (Proverbs 14:14).

A person could be perfect in his Bible reading, praying, and attendance of church services, do many wonderful works, and still be in a backslidden state.

The LORD sees all because **"the Lord looketh upon the heart"** (1 Samuel 16:7). **"For as he thinketh in his heart, so is he...."** (Proverbs 23:7).

This revelation—that God sees the very motive of our inner man—should drive us to seek Him in fresh repentance and diligence to guard our hearts. **"Keep** *(guard)* **thy heart with all diligence; for out of it are the issues of life"** (Proverbs 4:23).

If we do not take control of our thoughts, our thoughts will take control of us and lead to our eternal ruin. A pure heart is a requirement for eternal life in Heaven: **"Blessed are the pure in heart: for they shall see God"** (Matthew 5:8).

Who is going to **"see God"**? The **"pure in heart."**

> *"God wants our heart. Our motivations for things we do, mean a lot. WE must submit our will to God's will and be in a heart relationship with God. Actions matter, but so do motivations for our actions matter, but so do motivations for our actions."* –Shirley Bruso

See Philippians 4:8 and 1 Peter 1:13 for the divine prescription for the thought life.

> **"Finally, brethren, whatsoever things are true, whatsoever things are honest, whatsoever things are just, whatsoever things are pure, whatsoever things are lovely, whatsoever things are of good report; if there be any virtue, and if there be any praise, think on these things." Philippians 4:8**

Remember how the LORD forewarned us that on the Day of Judgment, there would be those who called Him **"Lord, Lord"** and then they will say things like **"have we not prophesied in thy name? and in thy name have cast out devils? and in thy name done many wonderful works?"** And yet, they will hear the horrific words of termination to their brutally eternal destination:

> **"And then will I profess unto them, I never knew you: depart from me, ye that work iniquity** *(lawlessness of heart)*.**" Matthew 7:23**

God have mercy upon me/us!

> **"Fear them not therefore: for there is nothing covered, that shall not be revealed;**

> **and hid, that shall not be known." Matthew 10:26**

God doesn't separate who we are in His sight from what we think upon. This is a critical issue to the LORD.

Here's more of His truth that reveals that the LORD sees us according to what we entertain in our hearts: **"For as he thinketh in his heart, so is he...."** (Proverbs 23:7).

Note that **"as he <u>thinketh</u>—so is he...."** Wow!

> **"And God saw that the wickedness of man was great in the earth, and that every imagination of the thoughts of his heart was only evil continually." Genesis 6:5**

Did you catch that? **"God SAW the WICKEDNESS...that every imagination of the thoughts of his heart..."** Here the LORD defines for us that **"wickedness"** is based upon **"the thoughts of the heart."** So, we see that one must not separate what he chooses to meditate upon in his heart, from what God sees and determines his state to be. He is either carnal/wicked, or spiritual (Christlike).

Am I **"carnally minded"** or **"spiritually minded"**? Such determines whether I am living in a spiritual state of **"death"** or **"life." "For to be carnally minded is death; but to be spiritually minded is life and peace"** (Romans 8:6).

We will eventually perform the things we give place to in our minds according to James 1:13-15. What should be realized is that although we will eventually perform the things we think upon, it doesn't take the physical act to offend the one true God (James 1:14-15; Matthew 5:28). Note in the verse above, that to be **"carnally minded"** is **"death"** (separation from fellowship with God). Note the word **"minded"** and the importance of this truth—it says nothing of physical performance (the act of sin/a transgression).

> **"This I say therefore, and testify in the Lord, that ye henceforth walk not as other Gentiles walk, in the vanity of their mind, Having the understanding darkened, being alienated from the life of God through the ignorance that is in them, because of the blindness of their heart: Who being past feeling have given themselves over unto lasciviousness** *(lawlessness)*, **to work all uncleanness with greediness. But ye have**

> **not so learned Christ; If so be that ye have heard him, and have been taught by him, as the truth is in Jesus: That ye put off concerning the former conversation the old man, which is corrupt according to the deceitful lusts; And be renewed in the spirit of your mind; And that ye put on the new man, which after God is created in righteousness and true holiness." Ephesians 4:17-24**

If I do not daily choose to walk the way of the cross (deny selfish desires) in the Spirit (the will of God; see Romans 8:1-14), then my heart will revert to type, which is revealed in many places in Scripture to be a state of wickedness before the LORD who is holy. Again, here is but one example:

> **"And God saw that the wickedness of man was great in the earth, and that every imagination of the thoughts of his heart was only evil continually." Genesis 6:5**

Defusing the iniquity of self-righteousness increases exponentially when we begin learning the biblical doctrine of fallen mankind and just how hopeless and evil we are outside of Christ (Genesis

6:5, 12; Isaiah 64:6; Jeremiah 17:9; Romans 7:18, 24; Psalms 39:4-5; Titus 3:5-7).

We must first realize that our hearts, without the divine influence of God's grace, are iniquitous, **"deceitful above all things, and desperately wicked"** (Jeremiah 17:9). Then, we must realize that this state of heart is condemned by the Almighty (Romans 8:5-8). Where are God's eyes pointed, looking? **"The LORD looketh on the heart"** (1 Samuel 16:7). Can God look upon a wicked heart and be pleased? **"Thou art of purer eyes than to behold evil, and canst not look on iniquity..."** (Habakkuk 1:13).

We cannot live in a wicked state of heart and be in fellowship with God who is holy. We cannot be grudging, unforgiving, lusting, or dwelling upon hatred, uncleanness, drunkenness, etc., and expect to maintain fellowship with the One who is holy by nature, holiness personified (holiest of all—no one else is as He is in His holy state of existence).

Since **"The LORD looketh on the heart"** and sees all (1 Samuel 16:7), there is no way of fooling Him, even when we may look good on the outside in the sight of men.

"Am I a God at hand, saith the LORD, and not a God afar off? Can any hide himself in secret places that I shall not see him? saith the LORD. Do not I fill heaven and earth? saith the LORD." Jeremiah 23:23-24

"The eyes of the LORD are in every place, beholding the evil and the good." Proverbs 15:3

"Be not deceived; God is not mocked: for whatsoever a man soweth, that shall he also reap." Galatians 6:7

"Neither is there any creature that is not manifest in his sight: but all things are naked and opened unto the eyes of him with whom we have to do." Hebrews 4:13

This disciple must become transparent in my heart toward God realizing that He sees all. All who don't will face severe and eternal consequences on that final Day. God will not permit any person to remain in His kingdom who continues to allow that which He condemns to permeate their minds (Psalms 101:4,7; Revelation 21:27, etc.).

What we think upon is a serious matter with the Most High. **"For as he thinketh in his heart, so is he"** (Proverbs 23:7).

Meditating on that which the LORD condemns, is sin, and Jesus came and died and **"condemned sin in the flesh"** (Romans 8:3; Matthew 5:28). See Colossians 3.

We should decide today to be honest. God is watching every thought and deed that we allow and perform, and He will judge us accordingly (2 Corinthians 5:10; Hebrews 4:12-13). O LORD help us. Have mercy upon us.

PRAYER: *Our dear heavenly Father, I come to You in Jesus' Name, afresh. Please search my heart and reveal that which does not please You. Grant this heart Your gift of repentance and to be a heart of flesh, pure, pliable, honest, teachable, humble, and ready to be corrected, changed, and transformed. In the name of Jesus Christ, Amen.*

Chapter 7

Authentically Seeking God in the Morning

"Be ready in the morning, and come up in the morning ... and present thyself." Exodus 34:2

More in a moment on Moses' morning meetings with the LORD.

We are engaged in a war for our own souls and those of others, and the battlefield where it all begins is in our own hearts, our own lives. Such is the land the LORD requires that we conquer first, and foremost. When I was a member of the U.S. Marines, our days began super early and without fail, were super productive. It is much the same being a member of the body of Christ, in that those who do not wake up swinging, are going to get knocked out. They're going to lose out. We have to own this reality, that we, as God's children, are in a fight, a war—like it or not. A war is raging over your life, for your eternal soul. And you are losing if you don't choose to begin your days diligently seeking the LORD.

The kingdom of God is a kingdom of conflict– **"And from the days of John the Baptist until now the kingdom of heaven suffereth violence, and the violent take it by force"** (Matthew 11:12).

We must love and honor our God **"first."** To seek the LORD **"first"** denotes priority–putting Him **"first"** and not ourselves. As we honor the LORD, there will be a leading to seek His holy face first thing each morning! When such is the case, the perfect will of God will pervade our lives. That is the promise of our LORD Jesus.

> **"But seek ye <u>first</u> the kingdom of God, and his righteousness; and all these things shall be added unto you." Matthew 6:33**

Putting Jesus first is literal. If we haven't settled in our heart, our life, to spend time with God daily (preferably first), we are backslidden, setting ourselves up for failure, doing things our own way instead of God's, and in utter need of repentance. Today is the day to turn back to Jesus as the **"first love"** of your life! See Revelation 2:4-5.

> *"I can do no good to those who come to seek from me if I have forgotten my time alone with God in the early morning."* –Robert Murray McCheyne

> *"In the past I would use the excuse that I wasn't awake enough to read. As a result, I had much less time with the Lord in His Word. Best to do it first. I have coffee every morning with Jesus and His Word."* –Meme A.

The disciple's day begins by talking with God in prayer and praise and thanksgiving and allowing Him to talk to us by studying his Word. A quality day with Jesus begins with communion with Him—first thing in the morning.

> *"The men who have done the most for God in this world have been early on their knees."* –E.M. Bounds

When God truly is first in your life, it's proven in that you arise each morning to seek His holy face, to do His holy bidding, to be led by His Holy Word and Spirit (Psalms 5:3; 63:1; Mark 1:35).

The LORD instructed His servant Moses to **"be ready in the morning, and come up in the morning ... and present thyself"** (Exodus 34:2).

Are you **"ready in the morning"**? Are you presenting yourself before the LORD in the morning? Is He your first priority when you awake? God instructed Moses:

> **"And be ready in the morning, and come up in the morning unto mount Sinai, and present thyself there to me in the top of the mount. 3 And no man shall come up with thee, neither let any man be seen throughout all the mount; neither let the flocks nor herds feed before that mount." Exodus 34:2-3**

Our meetings with God are to be private (Exodus 34:2; Matthew 6:6; Mark 1:35). He desires to meet with Him in private. To further emphasize this point, the LORD tells Moses that not even animals should be in the vicinity.

Those who choose to be **"ready in the morning"** to meet with God, will be ready when Jesus suddenly returns. For truly they are setting their heart affections upon Heaven's King instead of this world (Colossians 3:1-4).

> **"Let your loins be girded about, and your lights burning; 36 And ye yourselves like unto men that wait for their lord, when he will return from the wedding; that when he cometh and knocketh, they may open unto him immediately. 37 Blessed are those servants, whom the lord when he cometh shall find watching: verily I say unto you, that he shall gird himself, and make them to sit down to meat, and will come forth and serve them. 38 And if he shall come in the second watch, or come in the third watch, and find them so, blessed are those servants. 39 And this know, that if the goodman of the house had known what hour the thief would come, he would have watched, and not have suffered his house to be broken through. 40 Be ye therefore ready also: for the Son of man cometh at an hour when ye think not." Luke 12:35-40**

Think you really know Him? The person who does not have a daily prayer communion with the LORD has no oil in his lamp/vessel and is therefore not ready to meet Christ, the heavenly Bridegroom. Read Jesus' warning parable on the Ten Virgins in Matthew 25:1-13.

Satan is defeated as we are not only *positionally* but also *practically* dead, buried, and **"hid with Christ in God"** (Romans 6; Colossians 3:3).

There is no such thing in history as a powerfully used man or woman of God who was not given to our LORD in a life of prayer.

> *"Pray often; for prayer is a shield to the soul, a sacrifice to God, and a scourge for Satan."* –John Bunyan

> *"He who runs from God in the morning will scarcely find him the rest of the day."* –John Bunyan

> *"The secret place of prayer is the place to fight our battles and gain our victories."* –R.A. Torrey, *How to Pray,* p. 88

Moses was alone with God. Jesus did and taught the same: **"And in the morning, rising up a great while before day, he** *(Jesus)* **went out, and departed into a solitary place** *(uninhabited; no one else there)*, **and there prayed"** (Mark 1:35).

Note that when the LORD called Moses to meet with Him in the morning, he told Moses that He wanted personal time with him: **"no man shall come up with thee"** (Exodus 34:3).

Prayer is saving faith in action—the obedience of engaging in a personal perpetual, and intimate relationship with the savior. **"And this is life eternal, that they might know thee the only true God, and Jesus Christ, whom thou hast sent"** (John 17:3). In the divine economy and the personal life of every authentic disciple, knowing the LORD and a life of prayer are inseparable realities.

Isn't this private praying exactly what the same LORD Jesus taught us when instructing His disciples of the New Testament era on the important matter of prayer fellowship? Let's listen to our Savior:

> **"But thou, when thou prayest, enter into thy closet, and when thou hast shut thy door, pray to thy Father which is in secret; and thy Father which seeth in secret shall reward thee openly." Matthew 6:6**

As Exodus 34 continues, we will note here below that Moses went up as an empty blank slate, if you will. He met with God with no personal agenda. Perhaps this refers to the bless-ed humility in Christ's servant Moses, and therefore his openness to learn of the LORD. Moses was authentically humble and therefore teachable. He came up in the morning to meet with the LORD with a pliable heart and no preconceived notions or doctrines.

> **"And he hewed two tables of stone like unto the first; and Moses rose up early in the morning, and went up unto mount Sinai, as the LORD had commanded him, and took in his hand the two tables of stone. [5] And the LORD descended in the cloud, and stood with him there, and proclaimed the name of the LORD." Exodus 34:4-5**

Like Moses, are we allowing the LORD to be the Writer of the bless-ed constitution on our hearts? When we come before Christ with an open heart, He pens His Precepts upon our hearts, filling us with His Spirit. Speaking specifically of Moses, the apostle Paul writes:

> **"Nevertheless when it** *(a person's heart)* **shall turn to the Lord, the vail shall be taken away. [17] Now the Lord is that Spirit: and where the Spirit of the Lord is, there is liberty. [18] But we all, with open face beholding as in a glass the glory of the Lord, are changed into the same image**

from glory to glory, even as by the Spirit of the Lord." 2 Corinthians 3:16-18

After meeting with the LORD, Moses came out of that fellowship consumed with the Word and the Holy Spirit. Watch this:

"And it came to pass, when Moses came down from mount Sinai with the two tables of testimony in Moses' hand, when he came down from the mount, that Moses wist *(knew)* **not that the skin of his face shone while he talked with him. [30] And when Aaron and all the children of Israel saw Moses, behold, the skin of his face shone; and they were afraid to come nigh him." Exodus 34:29-30**

Just as Moses experienced, as they meet with Him, the countenance of the people of God today, will be lit—will shine bright for the world to see and take notice of the salvation of our God!

"Let your light so shine before men, that they may see your good works, and glorify your Father which is in heaven." Matthew 5:16

We cannot lead others where we are not willing to go ourselves. Moses arose in the morning to meet with God. He spent quality fellowship with the LORD. He sought God in private and was now being used of the LORD in public. Now he is **"hid with Christ in God"** (Colossians 3:3) and being used of the LORD to help others as our LORD desires to do in our lives.

> **"And Moses gathered all the congregation of the children of Israel together, and said unto them, These are the words which the LORD hath commanded, that ye should do them." Exodus 35:1**

Beloved, never again awake and do anything except seek God in your first moments. That's exactly how Jesus walked (Mark 1:35). For most of us, it would be self-deception to say that reading the Bible at night—as the very last thing you do—is going to cause you to grow in Christ, or even get done at all (Psalms 5:3). Would that be the equivalent of putting God *last* instead of *first*?

Our Mornings

During a season of ministry in my life, when 140 men had been thoroughly, individually ministered to and repented and received Jesus, with no exception, after each man gave his life to Jesus, discipleship began immediately. Deliberately and with deep conviction, I would look them directly in the eyes and lovingly, firmly say:

> *"Your day only begins right when it begins at the feet of Jesus! Whatever you do, read God's Word daily. From this day forward, never begin your day without reading, studying God's word and spending time with Him in prayer. It's more important than breathing and food. Don't ever begin your day, each and every day from now till eternity, without Jesus, without spending time in His Word and prayer."*

Beginning your day with Jesus—in His Word and prayer–assures being daily loaded with divine blessings.

> **"Blessed be the Lord, who daily loadeth us with benefits, even the God of our salvation. Selah." Psalms 68:19**

Is Jesus calling you to **"Be ready in the morning, and come up in the morning"**? See Exodus 34:2-3. Is the Savior bidding you to **"Come and dine"**?

> **"Jesus saith unto them, Come and dine. And none of the disciples durst ask him, Who art thou? knowing that it was the Lord." John 21:12**

Here we see Christ beckoning His disciples to **"Come and dine"** with Him. It was Jesus! He was calling them to sit and dine with Him! Gulp! Beloved of God, when you are prompted in your heart to **"come up in the morning"** to meet with the LORD, you can be assured it's not the flesh and it's not Satan but rather Heaven's glorious Bridegroom calling you to **"come and dine"** with Him. And we can know that it's going to be glorious as we hearken, when we come to Him as He prompts us.

Beloved, how can we possibly dish out if we don't first dine? How shall we feed if we don't first fellowship with Jesus? Is He calling us to answer His call to deepen and prioritize fellowship with Him?

> **"One thing have I desired of the LORD, that will I seek after; that I may dwell in the house of the LORD all the days of my life, to behold the beauty of the LORD and to enquire in his temple." Psalms 27:4**

> **"When thou saidst, Seek ye my face; my heart said unto thee, Thy face, LORD, will I seek." Psalms 27:8**

Recently, one lady rebuked me for preaching that disciples of Christ should seek His face in the morning, putting Him first. She said this was Americanized. Yet Jesus wasn't American, and neither was Moses or the Psalmist. This has nothing to do with what part of God's globe someone is living, nor era, but rather, that they are worshipping and looking unto the One who made all things and is our only salvation—according to His Word.

In this message we are looking at what Jesus and Moses said and did about early morning prayer, and it's clear that it was their custom to seek the LORD early in the morning—they put Him first:

> **"And <u>in the morning, rising up a great while before day, he</u>** (*Jesus*) **went out, and departed into a solitary place** *(uninhabited; no other man around)*, **and there prayed." Mark 1:35**

How did Jesus begin His days? Our LORD arose **"a great while before day"** and sought His Father. Are we following Jesus by beginning our day, every day, before His holy feet, seeking His beautiful face? If we are, we shall begin our days with Him (Mark 1:35; 1 John 2:6). **"He that saith he abideth in him ought himself also so to walk, even as he walked"** (1 John 2:6).

The Psalmist agrees: **"My voice shalt thou hear in the morning, O LORD; in the morning will I direct my prayer unto thee, and will look up"** (Psalms 5:3).

We have clear proof the LORD awoke His servant Isaiah early in the mornings. Isaiah wrote: **"The Lord GOD ... wakeneth morning by morning, he wakeneth mine ear to hear as the learned"** (Isaiah 50:4).

The psalmist wrote:

> **"O God, thou art my God; early** *(means 'dawn' in Hebrew)* **will I seek thee: my soul thirsteth for thee, my flesh longeth for thee in a dry and thirsty land, where no water is;" Psalms 63:1**

Did you know that **"morning"** appears 227 times in the King James Bible?

"Unless in the first waking moment of the day you learn to fling the door wide back and let God in, you will work on a wrong level all day; but swing the door wide open and pray to your Father in secret, and every public thing will be stamped with the presence of God." –Oswald Chambers

Mark Herridge Sr. writes, *"Give a man a prayer and he can have the victory today. Teach a man to pray and he can have the victory for a lifetime."*

Sister Debbie Lord shares:

"What blessed moments are those in the morning when bowing before the LORD God Almighty, magnifying Him—His ***'hallowed'*** *Name—holy, spotless, pristine, at once wonderful and terrible in His power and judgment, faithful in His mercy and love. The LORD God is more pure and true than any other thing or being in all of creation. There is none like Him. None can even begin to match Him in all of His majesty."*

PRAYER: *Heavenly Father, I come to You in the name of Jesus. Please captivate my heart with Your holy fear, to hasten my life to Your holy feet. Anchor my life in Your sweet fellowship. Please teach me to pray. Teach my heart concerning seeking Your holy face. Let my days begin with You, to be full of You, O God. I love You Jesus. Amen.*

Chapter 8

Dominating the Devil

"Jesus I know, and Paul I know; but who are ye?" Acts 19:15

Who are you? Does Satan know you? Does hell tremble when you awake in the morning? Only the authentic can dominate the Devil.

Can't Fool Satan

> **"And God wrought special miracles by the hands of Paul: [12] So that from his body were brought unto the sick handkerchiefs or aprons, and the diseases departed from them, and the evil spirits went out of them. [13] Then certain of the vagabond Jews, exorcists, took upon them to call over them which had evil spirits the name of the Lord Jesus, saying, We adjure you by Jesus whom Paul preacheth. [14] And there were seven sons of one Sceva, a Jew, and chief of the priests, which did so. [15] And the evil spirit answered and said, Jesus I know, and Paul I know; but who are ye? [16] And the**

man in whom the evil spirit was leaped on them, and overcame them, and prevailed against them, so that they fled out of that house naked and wounded." Acts 19:11-16

Can't Fool the LORD

"Be not deceived; God is not mocked: for whatsoever a man soweth, that shall he also reap. [8] For he that soweth to his flesh shall of the flesh reap corruption; but he that soweth to the Spirit shall of the Spirit reap life everlasting." Galatians 6:7-8

The LORD and His arch enemy know exactly who is authentic, and who is counterfeit (Acts 19:11-20).

Are you ready for deliverance, for the whole and complete victory that Christ alone died to give you?

How to Get the Devil Out of Your Life!

Is Jesus not the answer? Yes, He is. Let's give the world around us that answer to man's core dilemma—sin! Jesus is the only solution!

You can try to change your life by changing your thinking forever and never get delivered. A changed life requires God's grace through Christ and true repentance, obedience (Romans 12:1-2).

What Comes First?

"I beseech you therefore, brethren, by the mercies of God, that ye present your bodies a living sacrifice, holy, acceptable unto God *(absolute repentance)*, **which is your reasonable service. [2] And be not conformed to this world: but be ye transformed by the renewing of your mind, that ye may prove what is that good, and acceptable, and perfect, will of God." Romans 12:1-2**

We are being **"conformed"** to Christ, not this world.

The LORD is on a divine mission to kill us—to conform us to the image of the Son of God, and He's orchestrating all the things He allows in our lives to this very, exact, chief end and purpose (Romans 8:12-14, 28-29).

Marlene Austin notes:

"I said to the Lord a few years ago, 'Lord you're killing me.' He spoke in my spirit, 'Exactly—killing out the flesh so that I can shine through.' I wept then, I weep now, remembering the great love that swept over my soul! Oh, how I love Jesus."

Our hearts must be changed and only God Himself can do that. He desires to and will make that complete change in those who truly repent, lay down their life—door nail dead—seek His face, and follow Jesus.

"Love is the only true constrainer of our sinful nature and this love flows from Christ Himself in and through us. When we understand this, we should know that no one can overcome a sinful nature through will power and self-effort but only through Christ living through us." –Matthew Washington

Jesus Informed Us that We Have an Enemy!

Can you relate? Often the Holy Spirit prompts my heart to remember that the real battle rages in the

Spirit and not the flesh (Ephesians 6:12). Memorize this truth:

> **"For we wrestle not against flesh and blood, but against principalities, against powers, against the rulers of the darkness of this world, against spiritual wickedness in high places." Ephesians 6:12**

Jesus informs us that it is Satan who has come **"to steal, and to kill, and to destroy"** (John 10:10). Wherever you see stealing, killing, and destroying, you know that sin has given Satan legal ground to work His evil (James 4:7). Yet, Jesus then says, **"I am come that they might have life, and that they might have it more abundantly."** Here's Christ's enlightening statement:

> **"The thief cometh not, but for to steal, and to kill, and to destroy: I am come that they might have life, and that they might have it more abundantly." John 10:10**

Sin gives Satan the right to dominate one's life, yet Jesus came to **"destroy the works of the devil."**

> **"He that committeth sin is of the devil; for the devil sinneth from the beginning. For**

<u>this purpose the Son of God was manifested, that he might destroy the works of the devil</u>." 1 John 3:8

Note: you will never dominate the devil until you forsake all his wolves who pose as pastors. Discern: if he's not preaching repentance, the cross, hell, judgment, and holiness, he's a fraud! Run!

Freedom from Sin

- Any sin gives place to Satan (Ephesians 4:27; 6:11; James 4:7).
- The result of sin is death but through Jesus we have the forgiveness of sin (Ephesians 1:7).
- Sin brings death in the end if it is not repented of and forgiven (James 1:13-15; Ezekiel 33:12-13).
- Sin must be confessed, repented of, and forsaken (Proverbs 28:13; Luke 13:3; Acts 2:38; Acts 17:30; 2 Peter 3:9).
- Sin can be forgiven (Romans 6:23; John 8:32, 34; Acts 8:22; 1 John 1:9; James 5:16).

Jesus came to reunite us with the Father, to forgive and set free the captives of sin (Luke 4:18; Acts 3:26; 10:38, etc.). **"If the Son therefore shall make you free, ye shall be free indeed"** (John 8:36).

Christians must abide in Christ's Word, repent of sin, ask forgiveness, and pray for one another.

Who's ready to dominate the devil?

You cannot and will not dominate the devil until Jesus is dominating your own life—the cross! Such only happens when we **"reckon"** ourselves **"to be dead indeed unto sin, but alive unto God through Jesus Christ our Lord"** (Romans 6:11).

Learning the daily cross Jesus and His holy apostles instructed us to take up is essential to walking with Him (Luke 9:23-24; 2 Corinthians 4:10-12; Galatians 2:20; 5:24; 6:14; Colossians 3:4, etc.).

This life will not work without the cross—no matter what one tries. Having the cross in your personal life means Jesus will reign and God will bless and use you!

Bless-ed Deliverance and Victory is not for All

Jesus came ...

"To open their eyes, and to turn them from darkness to light, and from the power of Satan unto God, that they may receive forgiveness of sins, and inheritance among them which are sanctified by faith that is in me." Acts 26:18

"Ye are of God, little children, and have overcome them: because greater is he that is in you, than he that is in the world." 1 John 4:4

Only those who continue in the Word, in obedience to God, will be free from sin and Satan (John 8:31-32, 36). All those who are not doers of the Word are **"deceiving"** themselves and are under the control of the enemy of all souls (James 1:22).

"Then said Jesus to those Jews which believed on him, If ye continue in my word, then are ye my disciples indeed; [32] And ye shall know the truth, and the truth shall

make you free. ... [36] If the Son therefore shall make you free, ye shall be free indeed." John 8:31-32, 36

To be dominated by the Holy Ghost and dominate the devil, you must obey God. To hear and obey is essential (Isaiah 1:18-29).

Jesus came to bless abundantly and yet he will not unless His stated conditions are met. **"But be ye doers of the word, and not hearers only, deceiving your own selves"** (James 1:22).

We must obey the LORD and remember that just because God is using us, in no way means He's not still teaching, purging, chastening, correcting training, equipping, and stripping us. He's got bigger things in mind—even greater fruitfulness! **"Every branch that beareth fruit, he purgeth it, that it may bring forth more fruit"** (John 15:2).

"For Whom the Lord Loveth He Chasteneth"

No one said the purging, stripping, correction and chastening of the LORD isn't grueling and doesn't hurt—and yet, the LORD told us that these are necessary and that no son of His is without it. In fact, He says that anyone who rejects His work chooses not to be His—is without Him as their Father (Hebrews 12:5-11).

> **"And ye have forgotten the exhortation
> which speaketh unto you as unto children,
> My son, despise not thou the chastening
> of the Lord, nor faint when thou art
> rebuked of him: 6 for whom the Lord
> loveth he chasteneth, and scourgeth every
> son whom he receiveth. 7 If ye endure
> chastening, God dealeth with you as with
> sons; for what son is he whom the father
> chasteneth not? 8 But if ye be without
> chastisement, whereof all are partakers,
> then are ye bastards, and not sons.
> 9 Furthermore we have had fathers of our
> flesh which corrected us, and we gave
> them reverence: we not much rather be in
> subjection unto the Father of spirits, and
> live? 10 For they verily for a few days
> chastened us after their own pleasure; but
> he for our profit, that we might be
> partakers of his holiness. 11 Now no
> chastening for the present seemeth to be
> joyous, but grievous: nevertheless
> afterward it yieldeth the peaceable fruit of**

righteousness unto them which are exercised thereby." Hebrews 12:5-11

The LORD will do the following to those who cry out to Him for authenticity:

- strip
- rebuke
- chasten
- correct
- purge

Marlene Austin writes:

"Amen, we must endure the chastening of our Lord....it hurts, but I welcome it. It's amazing how you can feel His love all the while you are in pain. A thought: if Scripture tells us to train our children up in the way they should go, why would not our Father train us (His children) in the way we should go so that we will not depart from Him? Proverbs 22:6."

This disciple agrees with sister Marlene! I remember that same exact love, comfort, and safety I felt as a child when getting spanked and corrected for my wrongdoing. My father loved and therefore instructed me in the right way.

The remnant disciple of Jesus is known by his adherence to divine truth, Bible truth, no matter what the cost. He will **"endure hardness, as a good soldier of Jesus Christ"** (2 Timothy 2:3). This is in contrast with those the Holy Spirit warned us **"will not endure sound doctrine"** but will rather evade hard truths from the Word of God and those who preach the full counsel of it (2 Timothy 4:2-4).

The harshest of biblical truth is the delicacy, the delight of the true disciple of Jesus. He runs to all of it and never from any of it. He embraces the cross, never evading it. He delights in the sword of the Spirit that cuts to the core and carves the image of Christ into his life – into the fabric, the innermost core of who he is in Christ! Christ and the Christ alone is his sole identity, and he counts not his own life in this world dear unto himself so that he is able to finish his course with great joys–hearing from His Savior the sweetest of all words **"Well done, thou good and faithful servant ... enter thou into the joy of thy lord"** (Matthew 25:21; Acts 20:24; Romans 8:29; Galatians 2:20; 6:14; 2 Timothy 2:3).

Does God have a purpose in commanding you to train up and spank/correct your children? Yes, He does, and if you are an authentic disciple, you will obey Him without excuse in this matter. Just as the

LORD has His purposes to transform the lives of His own people, so He instructs us to **"train up"** our children for His purposes and glory (Proverbs 22:6).

On this important biblical topic of training up children and how it relates to His relationship with us, Gina Mondello writes:

> *"Oh yes I remember the spankings! It taught us early on who our authority was—not ourselves! It taught us to fear and respect authority which was only for our good to prepare us to fear, obey, and respect God, our ultimate Authority! It was a blessing to be spanked! Just look at what no spanking has produced today!"*

> *"It is doubtful whether God can bless a man greatly until He has hurt him deeply."* –A.W. Tozer

We must be purged to be prepared and **"meet** *(fit)* **for the master's use"** (2 Timothy 2:21).

> **"If a man therefore purge himself from these, he shall be a vessel unto honour, sanctified, and meet for the master's use,**

and prepared unto every good work." 2 Timothy 2:21

"The preacher's sharpest and strongest preaching should be to himself. His most difficult, delicate, laborious, and thorough work must be with himself. The training of the twelve was the great, difficult, and enduring work of Christ. Preachers are not sermon makers, but men makers and saint makers, and he only is well-trained for this business who has made himself a man and a saint. It is not great talents nor great learning nor great preachers that God needs, but men great in holiness, great in faith, great in love, great in fidelity, great for God - men always preaching by holy sermons in the pulpit, by holy lives out of it. These can mold a generation for God." –E.M. Bounds

Fake vs. Authentic

The counterfeit wants only to hear that which is convenient to him such as the promises of God—that which does not require true repentance, laying down their life in this fleeting world, and the denial of self (the crucified life). The tares know nothing of meeting the conditions for the promises of God because they simply refuse to repent, change, and die (John 15:7).

This is how the authentic and the counterfeit are discerned.

Authentic disciples of Christ migrate to His truth. They fall upon the stone, the sword of His Word to be broken and circumcised (Matthew 21:44; Ephesians 6:17; Hebrews 4:12). They study, embrace and **"endure sound doctrine"**—the whole of Holy Scripture (Acts 17:10-11; 2 Timothy 2:15; 3:16-17; 4:2-4). In contrast, the counterfeit migrates to false systems and cotton candy theology such as is being peddled in most local churches in this late hour (1 Timothy 4:1-2; 2 Timothy 4:2-4).

Those who **"turn away their ears from the truth"** of God, remaining religious and lukewarm, migrate to these counterfeit, un-biblical philosophies, false doctrines, and notions of ease which pervert the Gospel and the grace of God by refusing to preach the absolute necessity of true repentance, good fruit, good works, and a crucified and holy life (Luke 13:3; Acts 17:30; Hebrews 12:14; 1 Peter 1:15-16, etc.).

In a world of religious counterfeits who possess but a mere **"form of godliness,"** may God bless us to demonstrate true, authentic faith and worship-filled obedience to the nail-scarred risen LORD and Savior! (2 Timothy 3:5)

In Matthew 16, we read how Peter, one of Jesus' own 12, was used by Satan, just after he'd said to Jesus **"Thou art the Christ, the Son of the living God"** (Matthew 16:16). Then Peter sought to stop Jesus from going to the cross and Jesus said to him **"Get thee behind me, Satan: thou art an offence unto me: for thou savourest not the things that be of God, but those that be of men"** (Matthew 16:23).

Satan can use any of us just as he used Peter. Jesus is our only protection, and constant submission to Him is essential to keep the devil out.

> **"Wherefore let him that thinketh he standeth take heed lest he fall." 1 Corinthians 10:12**
>
> **"Neither give place to the devil." Ephesians 4:27**
>
> **"Be sober, be vigilant; because your adversary the devil, as a roaring lion, walketh about, seeking whom he may devour:" 1 Peter 5:8**

To keep the devil under foot, one must keep his own body under the power of the Holy Ghost, under subjection to the LORD, by way of the cross—the crucified life. When the death and burial is happening, so is the resurrection grace and glory of Christ raising that crucified and buried vessel upward! See 2 Corinthians 4:10-12.

> **"But I keep under my body, and bring it into subjection: lest that by any means, when I have preached to others, I myself should be a castaway." 1 Corinthians 9:27**

Greek for **"keep under"** is *hupōpiazō*: hoop-o-pee-ad'-zo. From a compound of G5259 and a derivative of G3700; to hit under the eye (buffet or disable an antagonist as a pugilist), that is, (figuratively) to tease or annoy (into compliance), subdue (one's passions).

Anyone willing to repent, to return afresh to the LORD can be delivered! Do you know what James 4:7 says? **"Submit yourselves therefore to God. Resist the devil, and he will flee from you"** (James 4:7).

Anyone who claims to be a Christian, yet rejects Christ's teachings, is not a Christian (John 8:47; 1 John 2:4).

Read James 4:7 again. Only those who submit to God on His stated terms—His written Word—will be able to **"resist** *(stand against)* **the devil"** and be free from him. This is a non-negotiable divine truth.

Today is your day to begin using the real Bible—the King James Bible. (See the post "Which Bible Can We Trust?" on SafeGuardYourSoul.com.

Did our LORD not announce to us what His divine mission was and still is?

Mission Statement of Jesus:

"The Spirit of the Lord is upon me, because he hath anointed me to preach the gospel to the poor; he hath sent me to heal the brokenhearted, to preach deliverance to the captives, and recovering of sight to the blind, to set at liberty them that are bruised," Luke 4:18

The only way to dominate the devil is to obey God by consenting to your own death, the crucified life.

"Always bearing about in the body the dying of the Lord Jesus, that the life also of Jesus might be made manifest in our body. [11] For we which live are alway

delivered unto death for Jesus' sake, that the life also of Jesus might be made manifest in our mortal flesh. [12] So then death worketh in us, but life in you." 2 Corinthians 4:10-12

If a person chooses not to love Jesus more than his own wicked self, that man will remain under Satan's control. Satan has influence and control over all who are not submitting to God (James 4:7). Jesus calls you to lay down your life—to die and let Him live and reign in you. Running from this cross message reveals that one is not honest, not authentic. Running to this repeated, biblically stated message of the original Gospel proves authenticity before God. Are you real?

Who do you desire to belong to? Wait no longer—go to Christ. Get to the cross, now!

"Ye are bought with a price; be not ye the servants of men" (1 Corinthians 7:23). Clearly, we have been purchased by the Blood of Jesus Christ. We are His property now. We belong to Him. As such, we are to serve Him and not mere men in this fallen world.

"Know ye not, that to whom ye yield yourselves servants to obey, his servants ye

are to whom ye obey; whether of sin unto death, or of obedience unto righteousness?" Romans 6:16

Simply knowing the truth is important and yet to walk in victory over the flesh, the world, and the devil, divine virtue must fill our lives—and that occurs through the daily cross life.

You really want to walk strong with God? Do this. You cannot and will not walk in total victory but will rather remain in sin and bondage until you lay down your life! Here is your opportunity to learn what the LORD says of this topic.

Who is ready for complete victory in Christ?

Here it is—The cross in action!

What Did Jesus Do to Combat Satan?

There is a lot of witchcraft going on in the name of spiritual warfare. Think: Just what did Jesus do when He combatted the devil? He simply quoted God's written Word which is final divine authority! (Read Matthew 4.) It is time to wise up and cease being led around by the nose by warlocks posing as Christ's ministers!

Message received:

"People like to say that we must wage war against Satan. The Bible is very clear that we must resist Satan, Jesus already won the war when he was crucified." –Maureen Lundie

Author's Reply:

"Good point and you bring to light the witchcraft of many 'ministries' that teach on 'spiritual warfare' and 'deliverance.' Perhaps it would be more biblical to say that in obeying God's command to be crucified with Christ and in putting on the full armor, Christ's victory is enforced in our lives, Satan is resisted and defeated (James 4:7). Jesus Christ already won the total victory when He single-handedly, by His own crucifixion, triumphed over Satan!"

"Blotting out the handwriting of ordinances that was against us, which was contrary to us, and took it out of the way, nailing it to his cross; 15 And having spoiled principalities and powers, he made a shew

of them openly, triumphing over them in it." Colossians 2:14-15

PRAYER: *Father in Heaven, please forgive my sin of unbelief, my evil heart of unbelief. Here and now, I return to You. I love You dear LORD Jesus and lay my life in Your holy hands here and now. Heavenly Father, please bless* this disciple *to be dead and buried with Christ and raised up in Your power dear LORD. In Jesus' Name.*

Chapter 9

Simply Authentic

"I have no greater joy than to hear that my children walk in truth." 3 John 4

How to Become an Authentic Disciple of Jesus Christ

Ask God for Help!

The Psalms are replete with David's cries to God for help throughout his life. To cite a few: **"Help me," "Teach me," "Show me," "Guide me," "Cause me," "Lead me."**

> **"Shew me thy ways, O LORD; teach me thy paths. 5 Lead me in thy truth, and teach me: for thou art the God of my salvation; on thee do I wait all the day." Psalms 25:4-5**

Here's what God said about David: **"I have found David the son of Jesse, a man after mine own heart, which shall fulfil all my will"** (Acts 13:22).

We don't have to guess as to the way which pleases God, we can know for sure—just ask Him! Open your Bible, your ears, your heart, and ask your LORD to show you His truth, to show you His way for your life.

> **"Ask, and it shall be given you; seek, and ye shall find; knock, and it shall be opened unto you: [8] for every one that asketh receiveth; and he that seeketh findeth; and to him that knocketh it shall be opened." Matthew 7:7-8**

> **"If any of you lack wisdom, let him ask of God, that giveth to all men liberally, and upbraideth not; and it shall be given him." James 1:5**

Believe That God Will Help You

> **"But without faith it is impossible to please him: for he that cometh to God must believe that he is, and that <u>he is a rewarder of them that diligently seek him</u>." Hebrews 11:6**

Know That the Holy Spirit Will Guide You

"Howbeit when he, the Spirit of truth, is come, he will guide you into all truth:" John 16:13

Make the Decision

King David was a man of great determination, many of whose decisions were recorded for us in the Book of Psalms: **"I will sing and give praise," "I will shout," "I will love thee," "I will trust," "I will call upon the Lord," "I will declare,"** and several more.

Insert your name here: I, ____________________, set my heart today, right now, to become an authentic disciple of Jesus Christ—by the will and grace of my LORD Jesus Christ!

Pray Simply—Simply Pray!

"But when ye pray, use not vain repetitions, as the heathen do: for they think that they shall be heard for their much speaking." Matthew 6:7

Remember, prayer is simply having a conversation with God—fellowshipping with Him in worship, praise, thanksgiving, repentance, singing, supplications, inquiries, listening to His leading, etc. **"Trust in him at all times; ye people, pour out your heart before him: God is a refuge for us. Selah"** (Psalms 62:8).

Pray to the Father in the name of Jesus: **"Verily, verily, I say unto you, Whatsoever ye shall ask the Father in my name, he will give it you"** (John 16:23).

When you come to the Father in the name of Jesus, you are approaching God the Father on His terms, via His **"one mediator between God and men"** —Jesus Christ (1 Timothy 2:5). And we know that God will hear you as He promised (John 14:13-14; 1 Peter 3:12). And we need to examine ourselves to make sure nothing is hindering our prayers such as:

- Unconfessed or un-forsaken sin—Isaiah 59:2; Proverbs 28:13
- Selfish motives —1 John 5:14
- Unbelief —James 1:6-7
- Unforgiveness —Matthew 6:14-15

Extremely strong emphasis is placed on prayer throughout God's Word. Having realized the importance that God places on prayer, someone observed that *"a true disciple of Jesus isn't described as having a prayer life but rather, having a life of prayer."*

Here are just a few Scriptures that highlight the place of prayer in the life of an authentic disciple:

- Pray always – Ephesians 6:18; Luke 18:1
- Be instant in prayer – Romans 12:12
- Pray about everything – Philippians 4:6
- Pray fervently – Colossians 4:12
- Pray without ceasing – 1 Thessalonians 5:17

"God is near at hand when you do approach Him in prayer. Oh, comforting truth! A God at hand to hear the softest breath of prayer-to listen to every confession of sin-to every cry of need-to every utterance of sorrow-to every wail of woe-to every appeal for counsel, strength, and support. Arise, O my soul! and give yourself to prayer; for God is near at hand to hear and answer you." – Octavius Winslow

So, instead of just mulling over your thoughts, be quick to turn to God in prayer. Let your mind, your thought life be filled with prayer.

"And be not conformed to this world: but be ye transformed by the renewing of your mind, that ye may prove what is that good, and acceptable, and perfect, will of God." Romans 12:2

The Word of God instructs us *how* to renew our mind, our thoughts:

"Finally, brethren, whatsoever things are true, whatsoever things are honest, whatsoever things *are* just, whatsoever things *are* pure, whatsoever things *are* lovely, whatsoever things *are* of good report; if *there be* any virtue, and if *there be* any praise, think on these things." Philippians 4:8

Be Forgiving

As you will see when reading the verses below, the act of forgiving others, or lack thereof, will have eternal consequences!

> **"For if ye forgive men their trespasses, your heavenly Father will also forgive you: [15] but if ye forgive not men their trespasses, neither will your Father forgive your trespasses." Matthew 6:14-15**

Read Jesus' parable in Matthew 18:21-35 which explains in no uncertain terms the necessity of forgiving others **"from your hearts."**

Deceit is the Opposite of Authentic—Repent!

God calls out deceitfulness as the number-one characteristic of the heart (**"above all things"**) and so it must be intentionally dealt with daily, diligently, and forcefully as our number-one enemy of being His authentic disciple. **"The heart is deceitful <u>above all things</u>, and desperately wicked: who can know it?"** (Jeremiah 17:9)

Who is the deceiver? The devil. **"For he** *(the devil)* **is a <u>liar</u>, and the father of it"** (John 8:44)! So, what spirit are we allowing to reside and operate in us if we host *any* deceit in our heart? The disciple must daily be sensitive as the Holy Spirit brings to light any trace, any speck of deceit, and the slightest impulse, thought or inclination to deceive.

We are in for a losing battle if we, without Christ and on our own, using our own human devices try to deal with the temptation to deceive (or *any* temptation for that matter). Jesus tells us to **"Watch and pray, that ye enter not into temptation: the spirit indeed is willing but the flesh is weak"** (Matthew 26:41).

> **"For we wrestle not against flesh and blood, but against principalities, against powers, against the rulers of the darkness of this world, against spiritual wickedness in high places." Ephesians 6:12**
>
> Why did Jesus come to the earth?
>
> **"For this purpose the Son of God was manifested, that he might destroy the works of the devil." 1 John 3:8b**
>
> **"Ye are of God, little children, and have overcome them: because greater is he that is in you, than he that is in the world." 1 John 4:4**

"Submit yourselves therefore to God. Resist the devil, and he will flee from you." James 4:7

It is impossible to over-emphasize the absolute necessity of thoroughly and relentlessly confessing before God, even the slightest tendency of deceit or thought of deception as it is brought to our attention. **"A little leaven leaveneth the whole lump"** (Galatians 5:9).

"Search me, O God, and know my heart: try me, and know my thoughts: [24] and see if there be any wicked way in me, and lead me in the way everlasting." Psalms 139:23-24

"Keep thy heart with all diligence; for out of it are the issues of life" (Proverbs 4:23). So, what will you allow to reside in your heart . . . deceit, or integrity, honesty and purity? Each of us decides this by how diligently we hearken to the LORD, and reject, renounce, and repent, confess all sin by the empowering grace of God, embracing death to self and the life of Christ (the crucified life). "**For ye are dead, and your life is hid with Christ in God"** (Colossians 3:3).

Don't stop reading here because this all sounds impossible to accomplish. Let's just agree up front that it *is* impossible ... without Jesus! Even the LORD's beloved apostle Paul cried out **"O wretched man that I am! who shall deliver me from the body of this death?"** (Romans 7:24).

Enter JESUS! **"For this purpose the Son of God was manifested, that he might <u>destroy</u> the works of the devil"** and **"that they might have life, and that they might have *it* more abundantly"** (John 10:10; 1 John 3:8b).

Hallelujah! God gives us grace sufficient for this life as we deny the self-life and become alive, raised up, in and by Christ (Galatians 2:20).

> **"There hath no temptation taken you but such as is common to man: but God is faithful, who will not suffer you to be tempted above that ye are able; <u>but will with the temptation also make a way to escape</u>, that ye may be able to bear it." 1 Corinthians 10:13**

Here's the **"way to escape"** that God in His faithfulness has made for us:

God multiplies His empowering grace and peace to us because we are known of Him (2 Peter 3:18). Jesus our LORD dwells within us along with His divine power to help us be godly in this life of glory and virtue that He has called us to!

> **"Grace and peace be multiplied unto you through the knowledge of God, and of Jesus our Lord, [3] <u>according as his divine power hath given unto us all things that pertain unto life and godliness, through the knowledge of him that hath called us to glory and virtue</u>: [4] Whereby are given unto us exceeding great and precious promises: that by these ye might be partakers of the divine nature, having escaped the corruption that is in the world through lust." 2 Peter 1:2-4**

You will find that being quick to recognize sin in your heart and repenting immediately, asking God's forgiveness for that specific sin, the instances of sin in your heart and mind will become less common. "**If we confess our sins, he is faithful and just to forgive us our sins, <u>and to cleanse us from all unrighteousness</u>**" (1 John 1:9). "**To forgive**" and "**cleanse**" completely ... that's powerful! The divine power of Christ at work in us!

When we were initially saved, God set us free from Satan's power over us that kept us in bondage to sin. Christ bought our freedom when He shed His perfect blood on the cross and cried out, **"It is finished"** (John 19:30).

So, we are no longer enslaved to Satan's power and have been given God's **"power that worketh in us"** (Ephesians 3:20), divine power to overcome all traces of sin that are part of our **"old man."** When we received Christ as our Savior, our soul was saved, but we still live in a human body and have the need to daily **"put off the old man with his deeds; And ... put on the new man, which is renewed in knowledge after the image of him that created him"** (Colossians 3:1-10).

The born-again disciple **"is a new creature: old things are passed away; behold, all things are become new. And all things are of God, who hath reconciled us to himself by Jesus Christ, and hath given to us the ministry of reconciliation"** (2 Corinthians 5:17-18).

This **"new creature"** in Christ is no longer *imprisoned and powerless* against the power of sin. Christ redeemed us by His shed blood and moved us from the captivity of darkness and death to the freedom of His light and life.

LORD, You made me Your new creature in Christ. Now please teach me, cause me, to greet, welcome and embrace the blessing of the crucified life so that You may increase and I may decrease. Raise up Your life in me so I can be filled more and more with your Spirit, love and light, righteousness and peace and joy in the Holy Ghost. In Jesus' Name I pray, amen.

Be a Person of Truth

"Sanctify them through thy truth: thy word is truth." John 17:17

"God forbid: yea, let God be true, but every man a liar; as it is written, That thou mightest be justified in thy sayings, and mightest overcome when thou art judged." Romans 3:4

When you are a person of truth, you will be communicating only God's truth by which the LORD makes men free! Read John 8:31-32, 36.

Those not honest with the Bible demonstrate that they aren't honest with its Author (Isaiah 5:20-24; John 8:47; 2 Timothy 4:2-4).

Be Accountable—to God First, and to the Other True Believers Around You

"Against thee, thee only, have I sinned, and done this evil in thy sight: that thou mightest be justified when thou speakest, and be clear when thou judgest." Psalms 51:4

"Let the righteous smite me; it shall be a kindness: and let him reprove me; it shall be an excellent oil, which shall not break my head: for yet my prayer also shall be in their calamities." Psalms 141:5

"Confess your faults one to another, and pray one for another, that ye may be healed. The effectual fervent prayer of a righteous man availeth much." James 5:16

Walk in the Light

"But <u>if</u> we walk in the light, as he is in the light, we have fellowship one with another, and the blood of Jesus Christ his Son cleanseth us from <u>all sin</u>." 1 John 1:7

"The entrance of thy words giveth light; it giveth understanding unto the simple." Psalms 119:130

As_we co-operate with God by daily laying down our lives before Him, dying to self and letting His power work in us (Ephesians 3:20), we are walking in AUTHENTIC DISCIPLESHIP!

"But we all, with open face beholding as in a glass the glory of the Lord, are changed into the same image from glory to glory, even as by the Spirit of the Lord." 2 Corinthians 3:18

"But that on the good ground are they, which in an honest and good heart, having heard the word, keep it, and bring forth fruit with patience." Luke 8:15

"Create in me a clean heart, O God; and renew a right spirit within me." Psalms 51:10

Be Consistent and Press On

The apostle Paul wrote the following about His own walk with Christ:

> **"Brethren, I count not myself to have apprehended: but this one thing I do, forgetting those things which are behind, and reaching forth unto those things which are before, [14] I press toward the mark for the prize of the high calling of God in Christ Jesus." Philippians 3:13-14**

Like Paul, the life of an authentic disciple can only be realized with an attitude of daily **"reaching forth"** and **press*(ing)* toward"** our God, seeking His holy face in praise, prayer and daily reading, study, and memorization of His Word. **"Sanctify them through thy truth: thy word is truth"** (John 17:17). **"Thy word is a lamp unto my feet, and a light unto my path"** (Psalms 119:105).

Let us remember that it is not our own human effort that will cause us to become an authentic disciple. **"For it is God which worketh in you both to will and to do of his good pleasure"** (Philippians 2:13). Rather, it is *our daily decision* to LET GO, DIE TO SELF and LET GOD have His way in us continually—the crucified life.

> **"I am crucified with Christ: nevertheless I live; yet not I, but Christ liveth in me:**

and the life which I now live in the flesh I live by the faith of the Son of God, who loved me, and gave himself for me." Galatians 2:20

"Humble yourselves in the sight of the Lord, and he shall lift you up." James 4:10

PRAYER: *Father in Heaven, I come to You in the name of Jesus Christ. Please make me pure and authentic to the core of my being. Strip every trace of falsity, and every erroneous notion, philosophy, and false doctrine from me. Instill in me Your holy fear and help me to be ever sensitive to Your voice and to be led by You in all things. Please establish and ground me in Christ dear Father and anoint me to be crucified and buried that You alone might reign in this life. You must increase but I must decrease LORD Jesus. In Jesus' Name. amen.*

Chapter 10

Having a Heart After the LORD

"But the LORD said unto Samuel, Look not on his countenance, or on the height of his stature; because I have refused him: for the LORD seeth not as man seeth; for man looketh on the outward appearance, but the LORD looketh on the heart." 1 Samuel 16:7

The LORD said that David was **"a man after mine own heart, which shall fulfil all my will"** (Acts 13:22).

The LORD is not hiding Himself from anyone, nor is He available to the merely casual seeker. If we don't have a heart after God today, all we have is dead religion—a mere form of godliness (Acts 13:22; 2 Timothy 3:5).

> **"One thing have I desired of the LORD, that will I seek after; that I may dwell in the house of the LORD all the days of my life, to behold the beauty of the LORD, and to enquire in his temple." Psalms 27:4**

Having a heart after God, a heart, a life that relentlessly seeks the LORD, is a choice—a wise choice being made today by all who are pressing into Jesus. Today we are either choosing to be full of self or full of Christ. Here's how we can be full of Christ: **"Blessed are they which do hunger and thirst after righteousness: for they shall be filled"** (Matthew 5:6).

By default, the person who is not fervently seeking Jesus today, is full of self, not Christ (Matthew 5:6).

"We would see Jesus," is the cry of every heaven-bound child of God (John 12:21).

When Samuel the prophet had examined all of Jesse's sons to see which one should be king in Israel, He passed by the tall, strong, handsome, established sons of Jesse to get to beloved David (1 Samuel 16:1-13). David had a superior quality that is rare. He is the only person in all the Bible called by God "a man after mine own heart."

> **"And when he had removed him** *(Saul)*, **he raised up unto them David to be their king; to whom also he gave testimony, and said, I have found David the son of Jesse, <u>a man</u>**

> **<u>after mine own heart, which shall fulfil all my will</u>." Acts 13:22**

The eyes of the Almighty are scanning the earth today, looking, searching for that one heart that pants after Him.

> **"For the eyes of the LORD run to and fro throughout the whole earth, to shew himself strong in the behalf of them whose heart is perfect toward him." 2 Chronicles 16:9**

The note below was found in the room of a young pastor in Zimbabwe, Africa, following his martyrdom for his faith in Jesus Christ.

> *"...I cannot be bought ... deluded or delayed. I will not flinch in the face of sacrifice, hesitate in the presence of the adversary, negotiate at the table of the enemy or meander in the maze of mediocrity. I won't give up shut up, let up until I have stayed up, stored up, prayed up, preached up for the cause of Christ. I am a disciple of Jesus. I must go until He comes, give till I drop, preach till all know and work till He stops me. And when He comes for His own, He will have no problem*

recognizing me … my banner will be 'Jesus, the Son of God.'"

May it be said of us, of you beloved of God, that you have a heart that is perfect toward your God, one that pants for more of Him daily.

Notice in 2 Chronicles 16:9 above, what the eyes of the LORD are searching for is the **"heart"** that is **"perfect toward Him"** and not *performance.* Wow! Selah. Meditate on that one. Your past performance means nothing to the LORD. What matters now, this moment, is whether or not you will turn your heart truly to Him and cry out to Him. **"My soul followeth hard after thee: thy right hand upholdeth me"** (Psalms 63:8).

As far as servant elders go, please remember that the true servant of the LORD will always foster in you an ever-deepening love for Jesus—a desire to know Him more (John 17:3; Philippians 3:10). The love for Jesus, resident in those with a heart after God, is contagious. They will never draw attention to themselves but only point all to Christ crucified as revealed in Holy Scripture! (Galatians 6:14; 1 Corinthians 2:2)

Religious or bloodline pedigree is zilch in Christ's kingdom (Matthew 20:20-28; 23:8-12). Our LORD aggrandizes the heart that follows hard after Him (2 Chronicles 16:9; Psalms 63:8).

Who would you rather spend a day with: a seminarian graduate, or a humble disciple with a heart after the LORD?

The seminary system is inept as well as the church system where people feel like they have sought God because they obtained a degree, or they attend a Sunday morning church service. Yet there is no fervency. There is no hunger or thirst to be found in them. They are lukewarm at best. This is tragic and will result in a spuing, a rejection (Revelation 3:15-16).

By biblical definition, the foolish virgins mentioned in Jesus' parable, are those who were once saved, espoused to the Bridegroom of Heaven, and have since fallen away from intimacy with Him. Their vessels are empty, and they will be shut out of His eternal bridal chamber if they don't repent and return to Him as **"first love"** (Matthew 25:1-13; Revelation 2:4-5).

> **"I know thy works, that thou art neither cold nor hot: I would thou wert cold or hot. 16 So then because thou art lukewarm, and neither cold nor hot, I will spue thee out of my mouth." Revelation 3:15-16**

Those who pretend to serve God, who treat Christ like a second- class citizen, serving Him only when it's convenient, reveal themselves to be self-serving, self-worshiping, self-idolatrous, lukewarm, backslidden, and hell bound.

Today is always the best time to repent, to lay down our life and obey God (Matthew 7:21; Revelation 22:14, etc.). The book of Revelation assures us that the fires of eternal damnation are going to forever feed upon the helpless, conscious souls of all who refuse to repent and return to Jesus as their **"first love"** (Revelation 2:4-5; 3:15-16).

Personally, I am constantly aware of the danger of the dehydration of the body and therefore continue to militantly force water into my body hourly. In the same way, and much more importantly, with eternal consequence, we must be disciplined followers of Christ who remain full of His divine virtue by perpetual fellowship. He warns us to **"pray without**

ceasing" (1 Thessalonians 5:17). **"Men ought always to pray and not to faint"** (Luke 18:1)

Those who don't drink lots of fresh water will lack in their health and those who don't drink from the well of the LORD in prayer without ceasing, will suffer spiritual defeat here and eternally (Matthew 26:41).

Talking to God in prayer is more important than our speaking to men about God (ministering). The greatest temptation we face is rejecting Christ, denying Him the **"first love"** place in our lives which includes our time, our hearts, and our lives in this temporal world (Revelation 2:4-5). Those who do not commune with the LORD in prayer, simply will not be imbued with His divine anointing to effectively, powerfully, overcome sin and Satan, and will also be empty of the divine virtue needed to minister to others.

> *"Jesus never taught His disciples how to preach, only how to pray. To know how to speak to God is more than knowing how to speak to people. Power with God is the first thing, not power with people. Christ loves to teach us how to pray."* – Andrew Murray, *With Christ in the School of Prayer*, pp. xxiii-xxiv

The disciples asked Jesus **"Lord, teach us to pray,"** not "teach us to preach" (Matthew 11:1).

Those not delighting in the LORD daily have self as their idol. **"Delight thyself also in the LORD; and he shall give thee the desires of thine heart"** (Psalms 37:4).

Are you lukewarm, fallen away, or are you one **"that stirreth up himself to take hold of thee** *(the LORD)*"? See Isaiah 64:7.

Beware of the Pitfalls

"Examine yourselves, whether ye be in the faith; prove your own selves. Know ye not your own selves, how that Jesus Christ is in you, except ye be reprobates?" 1 Corinthians 13:5

Those who examine and judge themselves, repenting, and bringing corrective action to their personal lives, will not be judged by God as the wicked will be. All who truly know God seek God and constantly examine themselves, taking honest inventory of their true spiritual state with the LORD.

> **"For if we would judge ourselves, we should not be judged. [32] But when we are judged, we are chastened of the Lord, that we should not be condemned with the world." 1 Corinthians 11:31-32**

Ultimately, we shall all stand before the LORD to give account and yet, that's not all the Bible says. Many isolate themselves from God's people and His Word spoken through His people (Acts 2:42; Colossians 3:16). They hide in darkness with the attitude that *"God will judge me so leave me alone"* because they are not accountable to Christ and therefore want no self-examination or the help of the body of Christ.

David said: **"Let the righteous smite me; it shall be a kindness: and let him reprove me; it shall be an excellent oil, which shall not break my head"** (Psalms 141:5).

"Reproofs of instruction are the way of life" (Proverbs 6:23b). Life in Christ involves continual learning, a never-ending classroom of divine instruction and correction, of learning to lay down our lives, to abandon ourselves to Christ—crucified with Him, dead and buried, and raised up by Him! Read 2 Corinthians 4:10-12.

We know our lives are not effectively dead and buried with Christ if the works of the flesh are raising their ugly head and manifesting! Read Galatians 5:16-24. So, we know then to get back to the cross, right?

"Whoredom and wine and new wine take away the heart" (Hosea 4:11). Sin takes away the heart. In other words, the reason some aren't full of holy conviction, fervent in spirit, full of the love, joy, and zeal of the LORD, is due to their own choice not to repent, be sanctified, and follow Jesus. Self and sin rule their lives, not Christ.

When a man truly repents, God takes away the stony, hardened heart caused by sin and gives him **"an heart of flesh"** (Ezekiel 36:24-26). Holy conviction returns.

> **"Wherefore seeing we also are compassed about with so great a cloud of witnesses, let us lay aside every weight, and the sin which doth so easily beset us, and let us run with patience the race that is set before us, [2] Looking unto Jesus the author and finisher of our faith; who for the joy that was set before him endured the cross, despising the shame, and is set down at the right**

hand of the throne of God." Hebrews 12:1-2

Greed is also a soul-damning sin often spoken of sin God's Word. Read 1 Timothy 6:6-17. Success is not money. No, true success is an abiding oneness, relationship with Jesus! Read chapters 15 and 17 in the Gospel of John.

"If ye then be risen with Christ, seek those things which are above, where Christ sitteth on the right hand of God. [2] Set your affection on things above, not on things on the earth. [3] For ye are dead, and your life is hid with Christ in God. [4] When Christ, who is our life, shall appear, then shall ye also appear with him in glory." Colossians 3:1-4

God promises that He will be found of us *only* if we seek Him deeply and diligently. **"But if from thence thou shalt seek the LORD thy God, thou shalt find him, if thou seek him <u>with all thy heart and with all thy soul</u>"** (Deuteronomy 4:29).

"Then shall ye call upon me, and ye shall go and pray unto me, and I will hearken unto you. [13] And ye shall seek me, and find me,

when ye shall search for me with all your heart. [14] And I will be found of you, saith the LORD: and I will turn away your captivity…" Jeremiah 29:12-14

"If thou seek him, he will be found of thee." 1 Chronicles 28:9

"When thou saidst, Seek ye my face; my heart said unto thee, Thy face, LORD, will I seek" (Psalm 27:8). By satanic design, today in the modern church building meetings, there seems to be little in the way of authentic worship and seemingly very little hunger for Christ (Matthew 5:6).

Life in Christ is Key

Here is something that has worked powerfully for me for many years. Is it biblical? Yes. (See the Bible verse below.)

Each evening, set yourself to get up in the morning to seek the LORD in His Word, praise, thanksgiving, and prayer. A nightly prayer to God and declaration to yourself could go something like….

"Dear Father, in Jesus' Name, if You choose to awake me in the morning, I shall seek You, I shall search, read, and study Your Word and seek Your holy face by delighting in prayer communion, thanksgiving, and praise. I love You Jesus!"

Meditate upon the following verse of divine truth and make it part of your life. **"Now SET your heart and your soul to seek the LORD your God"** (1 Chronicles 22:19).

Hebrew word for **"set"** – "*to apply, assign, cause, make, thrust, utter.*" With this definition of the word **"set"** in mind, read the above verse of Scripture again.

"Pray without ceasing" (1 Thessalonians 5:17). Begin every day with Christ!

Jesus says that in order to have the things of God added to your life, to have God richly present in your personal life, you must put Him first: **"But seek ye first the kingdom of God, and his righteousness; and all these things shall be added unto you"** (Matthew 6:33).

"First" in Matthew 6:33 means first priority. When God truly is first in your life, it's proven by arising each morning to seek His holy face, to commune with Him, to offer thanksgivings, to do His holy bidding, to be empowered and led by His Holy Word and Spirit (Psalms 5:3; 63:1; Mark 1:35). When He's first in your heart truly, He's first in your day!

> *"Each morning we are called by our heavenly Father to bring our whole selves before Him and His Word (1 Thessalonians 5:23-24). We must not be 'dull of hearing' (Hebrews 5:11) but be ready and eager to hear what He has to say in His Word and by His Spirit, even if it's a painful correction."* –Debbie Lord

PRAYER: *Heavenly Father, I want my life to glorify You, truly, authentically. Dear LORD there are so many inconsistencies in me that do not represent You that I now ask You to amend. Change me, please. Sanctify and anoint my life to be crucified with Christ, to be conformed to Your holy image dear LORD Jesus. I love You dear Master and Savior of my soul, my life. Holy Father, I ask these things in the name of Jesus Christ.*

Chapter 11

Mourning Vs. Mirth
Part One

The Two Houses: In Which House Are You Spending the Most Time?

"It is better to go to the house of mourning, than to go to the house of feasting: for that is the end of all men; and the living will lay it to his heart. [3] Sorrow is better than laughter: for by the sadness of the countenance the heart is made better. [4] The heart of the wise is in the house of mourning; but the heart of fools is in the house of mirth. [5] It is better to hear the rebuke of the wise, than for a man to hear the song of fools." Ecclesiastes 7:2-5

So many professing Christians today run from, evade all messages on repentance, the cross, and laying down their life in this fleeting world. As did the foolish virgins in Jesus' parable, we see today that many who were in their past espoused to the Great Bridegroom of Heaven are no longer anticipating and preparing for the wedding (Matthew 25:1-13). They are not following Jesus on HIS terms. No, they are living their best life now, having been coddled by the wolves who are using them (2 Timothy 4:2-4; 2 Peter 2:1-3).

It's sad that so few professors of Christianity are hearing and answering the call of God to come unto Jesus and serve Him on HIS terms, which always begins with true repentance and proving that repentance by bringing forth good fruit (Matthew 3:7-10). Many others have chosen a cheap counterfeit over the Son of God and are forfeiting the blessings of God in this life and the next.

Many want comfort and yet refuse Christ and the cross. **"For men shall be lovers of their own selves ... Traitors, heady, high-minded, lovers of pleasures more than lovers of God;"** (2 Timothy 3:1, 4).

When we spend time in the house of mourning (the cross-death, burial), the house, the place of mirth (celebration, resurrection) follows—awaits us! Shall we read this important passage again?

> **"It is better to go to <u>the house of mourning</u>** *(lamentation, sadness, grief)*, **than to go to <u>the house of feasting</u>: for that is the end of all**

men; and the living will lay it to his heart. [3] Sorrow is better than laughter: for by the sadness of the countenance the heart is made better.[4]The heart of the wise is in the house of mourning; but the heart of fools is in the house of mirth *(celebration, glee, gladness, rejoicing, festival).*" **Ecclesiastes 7:2-4**

Think Jesus' parable of the ten virgins (Matthew 25:1-13). It's for the love of her bridegroom-to-be that the espoused virgin forgoes running with the foolish virgins, the party-ers. Her love for her husband-to-be and fear of losing him are her healthy, warranted and wise inspirations.

This is an amazing revelation: Watch what King Solomon says here below. Foregoing self-serving gratification, feasting, celebration, always results in experiencing the death, the burial, and the resurrection joy and fulfillment that God alone can and desires to delight us with as we do things His way—by the cross. The cross, the death and burial (house of mourning) always precedes **"the house of mirth."**

"The house of feasting: for that is the end of all men" (v. 2): Pride was the root cause of the fall of Lucifer and a third of the angels of God in Heaven, and every civilization of mankind that has come and gone was destroyed in their pride-filled rebellion. Perhaps Sodom and Gomorrah are the most popular biblical example (Ezekiel 16:49-51).

The Wise and the Foolish Contrasted

Notice: **"The heart of the wise is in the house of mourning; but the heart of fools is in the house of mirth"** (v. 4). When divine wisdom begins to take up more real estate in our hearts, we begin to realize that His wisdom teaches us to get down low, into the death and burial, while foolishness tempts us to seek out **"the house of mirth,"** to excessively indulge in celebration—to "medicate" instead of walking through the loneliness and trial with the LORD and thereby being healed, made whole, prepared and matured (1 Peter 5:10).

We shall never experience God on the mountain as we will in the valley. When we "take it on the chin," we get knocked down, humbled low. This puts us in the place of weakness and God in the place of strength, ruling in us with His divine might!

> **"And lest I should be exalted above measure through the abundance of the**

revelations, there was given to me a thorn in the flesh, the messenger of Satan to buffet me, lest I should be exalted above measure. [8] For this thing I besought the Lord thrice, that it might depart from me. [9] And he said unto me, My grace is sufficient for thee: for my strength is made perfect in weakness. Most gladly therefore will I rather glory in my infirmities, that the power of Christ may rest upon me. [10] Therefore I take pleasure in infirmities, in reproaches, in necessities, in persecutions, in distresses for Christ's sake: for when I am weak, then am I strong." 2 Corinthians 12:7-10

So many clueless parents today are destroying their own children by filling them with sugary desserts when the child isn't being made responsible to eat the meat and vegetables. In the same way, false leaders today are spiritually, eternally assassinating their gullible, biblically illiterate audiences by feeding them the cotton candy "best life now" gospel instead of teaching them the cross—the crucified life—of the original Gospel of Jesus (2 Timothy 4:2-4).

Our LORD Jesus suffered greatly in **"the house of mourning."** The divine resurrection followed the mourning, the great suffering of our Savior.

> **"He is despised and rejected of men; a man
> of sorrows, and acquainted with grief: and
> we hid as it were our faces from him; he
> was despised, and we esteemed him not. 4
> Surely he hath borne our griefs, and
> carried our sorrows: yet we did esteem him
> stricken, smitten of God, and afflicted. 5
> But he was wounded for our
> transgressions, he was bruised for our
> iniquities: the chastisement of our peace
> was upon him; and with his stripes we are
> healed. 6 All we like sheep have gone
> astray; we have turned every one to his
> own way; and the LORD hath laid on him the
> iniquity of us all. 7 He was oppressed, and
> he was afflicted, yet he opened not his
> mouth: he is brought as a lamb to the
> slaughter, and as a sheep before her
> shearers is dumb, so he openeth not his
> mouth. 8 He was taken from prison and
> from judgment: and who shall declare his
> generation? for he was cut off out of the
> land of the living: for the transgression of
> my people was he stricken. 9 And he made**

his grave with the wicked, and with the rich in his death; because he had done no violence, neither was any deceit in his mouth. [10] Yet it pleased the LORD to bruise him; he hath put him to grief: when thou shalt make his soul an offering for sin, he shall see his seed, he shall prolong his days, and the pleasure of the LORD shall prosper in his hand. [11] He shall see of the travail of his soul, and shall be satisfied: by his knowledge shall my righteous servant justify many; for he shall bear their iniquities. [12] Therefore will I divide him a portion with the great, and he shall divide the spoil with the strong; because he hath poured out his soul unto death: and he was numbered with the transgressors; and he bare the sin of many, and made intercession for the transgressors." Isaiah 53:3-12

"The only way to promotion is by demotion. Are you today seeking a demotion? Do you want self to be advanced, enhanced, prominent, recognized, satisfied, aggrandized, indulged, promoted, noticed or applauded? Or do you want self to be demoted, crucified, and killed to all these worldly things?" –Travis Bryan III

The biblical truth of the greatest severity—the cross life—is also the most precious and satisfying for Jesus' true disciple who will run to it and not from it. He will embrace it and never evade it. He delights in the sword of the Spirit that cuts to the heart of his being, conforming him to the image of Christ–all the way to the very core, the innermost essence of who he is in Christ!

Going to church, church membership is the religion of many today. They love the ease of it because it never demands true repentance with good works to prove that the repentance is real (Matthew 3:7-10).

Jesus specifically, in detail, warns us of the dangers, the eternal danger of soul, associated with **"the house of mirth,"** the life of ease, when He says:

> **"And take heed to yourselves, lest at any time your hearts be overcharged with surfeiting, and drunkenness, and cares of this life, and so that day come upon you unawares. [35] For as a snare shall it come on all them that dwell on the face of the whole earth. [36] Watch ye therefore, and pray always, that ye may be accounted worthy to**

escape all these things that shall come to pass, and to stand before the Son of man." Luke 21:34-36

The life of over-indulgence will always lead to eternal damnation. **"But she that liveth in pleasure is dead while she liveth"** (1 Timothy 5:6).

Jesus warns:

"Enter ye in at the strait gate: for wide is the gate, and broad is the way, that leadeth to destruction, and many there be which go in thereat: [14] Because strait is the gate, and narrow is the way, which leadeth unto life, and few there be that find it." Matthew 7:13-14

Jesus is now, again reigning as supreme LORD at the right hand of the Father, having accomplished the cross, redemption through His death, burial, and resurrection.

"And being found in fashion as a man, he humbled himself, and became obedient unto death, even the death of the cross. [9] Wherefore God also hath highly exalted

him, and given him a name which is above every name:" Philippians 2:8-9

Based on His earthly sufferings, our Messiah is rightly called "the suffering Servant" (Isaiah 53, etc.). Jesus suffered, died, was buried, and raised again from the dead. He calls us to also suffer the death of self that He might exalt us in His resurrection power, for His glory.

"Forasmuch then as Christ hath suffered for us in the flesh, arm yourselves likewise with the same mind: for he that hath suffered in the flesh hath ceased from sin;
2 That he no longer should live the rest of his time in the flesh to the lusts of men, but to the will of God." 1 Peter 4:1-2

Suffering our own death to self so that Christ is reigning, is the Gospel in action in our personal lives. **"For unto you it is given in the behalf of Christ, not only to believe on him, but also to suffer for his sake"** (Philippians 1:29).

Suffering for Christ is a reality of the original Gospel, though seldom if ever mentioned in the modern church world.

Adversity is the greatest classroom for learning, not comfort and ease.

> *"Embrace the cross sufferings: embrace confusion, darkness, sinking and falling—fall into God, hold your pain, marinate in your suffering. If love can't change it, accept it. Present your body as a living sacrifice to death downs and resurrection ups with Christ. Run toward the cross, not away from it or try to escape it. Begin to see bad things you don't deserve as positive things. View everything that happens in life as win/win. Bad is good. Good is good! Realize that to embrace suffering is to embrace the destruction of your main enemy: the egocentric self!"* –Travis Bryan III

When Israel was in rebellion, the LORD warned that He was going to remove the mirth from them:

> **"Then will I cause to cease from the cities of Judah, and from the streets of Jerusalem, the voice of mirth, and the voice of gladness, the voice of the bridegroom, and the voice of the bride: for the land shall be desolate." Jeremiah 7:34**

Jesus is going to judge all men and eternally remove all **"mirth,"** that is, all joy, bliss, and celebration from the wicked—those who refuse to mourn for their sins in true repentance and faith and be saved (James 4:6-10).

"Blessed are they that mourn: for they shall be comforted" (Matthew 5:4). Those who mourn in this life are already experiencing a foretaste of glory divine—comfort from the **"God of all comfort"** (2 Corinthians 1:2-5).

Serendipity: You really don't begin to enjoy your life in this world until you lay it down—do it God's way and not your own (Matthew 6:33; Luke 9:23-24; 14:33; 17:33). Every true disciple can testify to this.

No, I didn't just speak of or even hint at loving this world (1 John 2:15). Yet, having a clear conscience and deep inner peace granted by God Himself is essential to the fulfillment that glorifies Christ (Psalms 23).

Those in Christ will suffer and mourn and weep in this life: **"Ye shall weep and lament, but the world shall rejoice: and ye shall be sorrowful ..."** and yet, in the end **"your sorrow shall be turned into joy"** (John 16:20).

"For his anger endureth but a moment; in his favour is life: weeping may endure for a night, but joy cometh in the morning." Psalms 30:5

"For which cause we faint not; but though our outward man perish, yet the inward man is renewed day by day. [17] For our light affliction, which is but for a moment, worketh for us a far more exceeding and eternal weight of glory; [18] While we look not at the things which are seen, but at the things which are not seen: for the things which are seen are temporal; but the things which are not seen are eternal." 2 Corinthians 4:16-18

PRAYER: *LORD, please bless my spirit to be temperate, to be sober, to be wholly dependent upon You. Please help me to rest in You and to immediately and always walk in the Holy Spirit, thanking You and rejoicing in and for all tribulations which work patience and maturity in this life. Thank You Jesus for conforming my life into Your holy image. In Jesus' Name. Amen.*

Chapter 12

Mourning Vs. Mirth
Part Two

The Two Houses: In Which House Are You Spending the Most Time?

"But he giveth more grace. Wherefore he saith, God resisteth the proud, but giveth grace unto the humble. [7] Submit yourselves therefore to God. Resist the devil, and he will flee from you. [8] Draw nigh to God, and he will draw nigh to you. Cleanse your hands, ye sinners; and purify your hearts, ye double minded. [9] Be afflicted, and mourn, and weep: let your laughter be turned to mourning, and your joy to heaviness. [10] Humble yourselves in the sight of the Lord, and he shall lift you up." James 4:6-10

In Christ's kingdom, here and now, there is the need to **"Be afflicted, and mourn, and weep: let your laughter be turned to mourning, and your joy to heaviness."**

There are deaths, burials, and resurrections in our lives. There cannot be the resurrection (mirth) until there is first the death and burial (the mourning). The following passage from 2 Corinthians 4 gives us the rhythm of the cross life in the divine economy. May God bless each of us to get in on this Gospel action! Pouring prayerfully over these divinely inspired words is sure to be instrumental in bringing about God's will in our lives.

> **"Always bearing about in the body the dying of the Lord Jesus, that the life also of Jesus might be made manifest in our body.**
> **11 For we which live are alway delivered unto death for Jesus' sake, that the life also of Jesus might be made manifest in our mortal flesh. 12 So then death worketh in us, but life in you." 2 Corinthians 4:10-12**

Only through the cross lifestyle can the disciple experience practically the riches of Christ.

Let us **"taste and see that the LORD is good"** as we forgo our own idea of feasting, excessive celebration of the things of this world, and get down low in worshipful humility, sinking down deep into the death of Christ and allowing God to bring us upward into His lavish chambers of fruitful delight, a foretaste of glory divine! **"O taste and see that the LORD is good: blessed is the man that trusteth in him"** (Psalms 34:8).

In Ecclesiastes 7, Solomon is in no way saying that celebration is wrong and yet, allowing God to fill our hearts with His resurrection joy and occasions of celebration is infinitely sweeter than doing things our own way by perpetually avoiding pain and mourning—death and burial—in order to seek out celebration. **"Thou wilt shew me the path of life: in thy presence is fulness of joy; at thy right hand there are pleasures for ever more"** (Psalms 16:11).

Israel's history recorded in the Bible is laden with repeated rebellion and they suffered greatly for it. The celebration of the people of God followed great suffering, as God liberated them. When the LORD set Israel free, releasing them from the bondage of enemy nations, such as Babylon, they **"were like them that dream,"** and instructed by God to be fruitful for His glory.

Psalm 126

"A Song of degrees. When the LORD turned again the captivity of Zion *(set them free)*, **we**

were like them that dream. [2] Then was our mouth filled with laughter, and our tongue with singing: then said they among the heathen, The LORD hath done great things for them. [3] The LORD hath done great things for us; whereof we are glad. [4] Turn again our captivity, O LORD, as the streams in the south. [5] They that sow in tears shall reap in joy. [6] He that goeth forth and weepeth, bearing precious seed, shall doubtless come again with rejoicing, bringing his sheaves with him."

"Turned - Brought the captive Israelites out of Babylon into their own land. Dream - We were so surprised and astonished." –John Wesley

Message received: *"I think one needs to go through some stuff to really appreciate life and understand what it means to persevere, overcome and have faith."*

Author's response: *"Totally agree by experience, and these passages demonstrate this truth: 1 Peter 5:10; James 1:2-4 and Ecclesiastes 7:1-8."*

Throughout Israel's history, after receiving victory, God's people would later become unthankful, unholy, doing things their own way instead of God's and overly indulge in **"the house of mirth."** They were therefore allowed to be led back into slavery, under the bondage of the enemy.

Jesus teaches that each individual whom He saves must **"deny himself, and take up his cross daily, and follow me. [24] For whosoever will save his life shall lose it: but whosoever will lose his life for my sake, the same shall save it"** (Luke 9:23-24).

The believer is to live an abiding life with Christ, bearing the fruit that testifies to such (John 15). The Bible is full of warnings concerning falling away (Luke 8:13). If falling away were not possible, no such warnings would exist in Holy Writ.

> **"Therefore we ought to give the more earnest heed to the things which we have heard, lest at any time we should let them slip. [2] For if the word spoken by angels was stedfast, and every transgression and disobedience received a just recompence of reward; [3] How shall we escape** *(eternal judgment)*, **if we neglect so great salvation; which at the first began to be spoken by the**

Lord, and was confirmed unto us by them that heard him;" Hebrews 2:1-3

On a personal note: In the past, I could never and had never been possessed by the deep satisfaction and fulfillment that now fills my life as I choose to do things God's way, and not my own. The cross is God's way. Every disciple reading this, who is learning that cross truth, can certainly concur!

"Better is the end *(resurrection)* **of a thing than the beginning thereof** *(death and burial):* **and the patient in spirit is better than the proud in spirit." Ecclesiastes 7:8**

Surely the resurrection is better, more pleasurable than the death and burial, the dying, and yet the resurrection *cannot occur* without the death and burial first happening.

Adam Clarke on Ecclesiastes 7:2:

"It is better to go to the house of mourning - Birthdays were generally kept with great festivity, and to these the wise man most probably refers; but according to his maxim, the miseries of life were so many and so oppressive that the day of a man's death was to be preferred

to the day of his birth. But, independent of the allusion, it is much more profitable to visit the house of mourning for the dead than the house of festivity. In the former we find occasion for serious and deeply edifying thoughts and reflections; from the latter we seldom return with one profitable thought or one solid impression."

Adam Clarke on Ecclesiastes 7:4:

"The heart of the wise is in the house of mourning - A wise man loves those occasions from which he can derive spiritual advantage; and therefore prefers visiting the sick, and sympathizing with those who have suffered privations by death. But the fool - the gay, thoughtless, and giddy - prefers places and times of diversion and amusement. Here he is prevented from seriously considering either himself or his latter end. The grand fault and misfortune of youth."

"I walked a mile with Pleasure;
She chatted all the way.
But left me none the wiser
For all she had to say
I walked a mile with Sorrow,
And not a word said she;
But oh, the things I learned from her

When sorrow walked with me"
—Robert Browning Hamilton

"And he lifted up his eyes on his disciples, and said, Blessed be ye poor: for yours is the kingdom of God. 21 Blessed are ye that hunger now: for ye shall be filled. Blessed are ye that weep now: for ye shall laugh. 22 Blessed are ye, when men shall hate you, and when they shall separate you from their company, and shall reproach you, and cast out your name as evil, for the Son of man's sake. 23 Rejoice ye in that day, and leap for joy: for, behold, your reward is great in heaven: for in the like manner did their fathers unto the prophets. 24 But woe unto you that are rich! for ye have received your consolation. 25 Woe unto you that are full! for ye shall hunger. Woe unto you that laugh now! for ye shall mourn and weep. 26 Woe unto you, when all men shall speak well of you! for so did their fathers to the false prophets." Luke 6:20-26

Beloved of God, may we no longer run from the pain associated with dying to self. Instead, let us embrace it, for therein, in our own demise, is the supreme reign of Christ.

Concerning our dying to self and the resulting heavenly treasure, Travis Bryan III writes:

"In the cross:
. . . freedom from self comes forth.
. . . new creation comes forth.
. . . new perspective comes forth.
. . . transformation by a renewed mind comes forth.
. . . glory (or 'weight of glory') is realized.
. . . immunity (or resurrection immunity) to pain is realized.

"The only real way to escape pain is to embrace it. It only gets worse when one uses human ways to numb it or escape it, pass it on or put it off on someone else."

"Therefore also now, saith the LORD, turn ye even to me with all your heart, and with fasting, and with weeping, and with mourning:" Joel 2:12

PRAYER: *Holy Father, in the name of Jesus, please forgive my sins, namely murmuring, spiritual adultery, idolatry, and unbelief. Father, please break me to the core of this being You made. Anoint my life to be truly crucified with Christ and thankful in all things, knowing You are working in my life and through all the trials and tribulations that You allow. In Jesus' Name, amen.*

Chapter 13

Joy Comes After the Mourning

"Deep calleth unto deep at the noise of thy waterspouts: all thy waves and thy billows are gone over me." Psalms 42:7

All those who desire Christ's deeper work, deeper life truths manifesting in their personal life, desire a good and godly thing.

"Make me Your authentic disciple," is the cry to the LORD of every true saint of Christ.

As we see in Psalms 30:5 and other Bible verses, joy cometh in the *mourning*. Many times, the rich joy of the LORD does not come in the seasons of **"mirth,"** or comfort, ease, or times of celebration. Rather, joy is born in times of testing as we trust God in adversity—in the **"mourning"**—the times of trials, tribulation, testing, persecution, purging, suffering, chastening, humbling, and adversity.

Message Received:

"The word of faith and NAR movements are not preparing the people for tribulation - and as a

result the people will fall away during real hard times because they won't believe the Lord would allow them to go through such things." –Connie Russo

Author's reply:

"Exactly! The people who sit under the many false shepherds are not ready to meet Christ. Due to my indoctrination with the heresies of the Word of faith, NAR cults, in the early days of being saved, the LORD had to undo these lies. It's taken decades. This is the process the LORD had to bring me through personally—to allow ongoing sufferings to come upon my life and teach me that truly following Him involves ***'MUCH tribulation'*** *(Acts 14:22). Suffering only proves one is truly saved (Matthew 11:12; James 1:2-4; 1 Peter 4:12-14, etc.). And Christ's saints are to rejoice and know they are* ***'blessed'*** *to be persecuted for Christ's sake!"*

"Blessed are they which are persecuted for righteousness' sake: for theirs is the kingdom of heaven. 11 Blessed are ye, when men shall revile you, and persecute you, and shall say all manner of evil against you falsely, for my sake. 12 Rejoice, and be

exceeding glad: for great is your reward in heaven: for so persecuted they the prophets which were before you." Matthew 5:10-12

In Christ's Kingdom, the Only Way Up is Down

In Christ's kingdom, the only way up is down, and sufferings—death and burial.

As we worship, seek, and serve the LORD, no matter what trials come our way, Joy comes *in* the mourning and thereafter!

"Draw nigh to God, and he will draw nigh to you. Cleanse your hands, ye sinners; and purify your hearts, ye double minded. [9] Be afflicted, and mourn, and weep: let your laughter be turned to mourning, and your joy to heaviness *(the cross)*. **[10] Humble yourselves in the sight of the Lord, and he shall lift you up** *(resurrection)*.**" James 4:8-10**

"For his anger *(for our sin)* **endureth but a moment; in his favour is life: weeping may**

endure for a night, but joy cometh in the morning." Psalms 30:5

Adversity is the greatest classroom for learning, not comfort and ease.

"Wherein ye greatly rejoice, though now for a season, if need be, ye are in heaviness through manifold temptations: [7] that the trial of your faith, being much more precious than of gold that perisheth, though it be tried with fire, might be found unto praise and honour and glory at the appearing of Jesus Christ." 1 Peter 1:6-7

The LORD is so gracious that He gives us His joy during and after seasons of weeping/mourning.

"Thou hast turned for me my mourning into dancing: thou hast put off my *sackcloth* *(concerns a time of repentance)* and girded me with gladness." Psalms 30:11

Here we see how God clothes His people with His righteousness as they come before Him in true repentance.

If I am not truly seeking the face of the LORD, engaging daily in the life-giving abiding relationship He desires, I am simply going through religious motions, have a hardened heart, and a mere **"form of godliness"** (1 Chronicles 16:11; Psalms 27:4, 8; Philippians 3:10 and 2 Timothy 3:5).

Hosea 10:12 comes to mind: **"Sow to yourselves in righteousness, reap in mercy; break up your fallow ground: for it is time to seek the LORD, till he come and rain righteousness upon you"** (Hosea 10:12).

Drawing close to God begins at repentance and receiving Jesus the moment He saves us. And yet, continually drawing close to the LORD thereafter, after initial salvation, is taught throughout Scripture and is essential in the abiding relationship Jesus ordained for each of His children (John 15). Let's read this extremely important passage again. To His own, through James, the LORD beckons:

> **"Draw nigh to God, and he will draw nigh to you. Cleanse your hands, ye sinners; and purify your hearts, ye double minded. [9] Be afflicted, and <u>mourn</u>, and weep: let your laughter be turned to mourning, and your joy to heaviness** *(the cross)*. **[10] Humble**

> **yourselves in the sight of the Lord, and he shall lift you up** *(resurrection)***." James 4:8-10**

Being **"double minded"** would mean to be other than armed with the mind of Christ, cross-minded. You must consent to the death of your own will before the LORD will fill you with faith and raise you upward in His grace to do His will.

Is it not in the place of affliction that our hearts are opened to truly learn, to be made fertile–for the Word to be truly engrafted into our lives? As we are blessed to walk through seasons of trials, the divine grace will be present to **"lay apart all filthiness and superfluity of naughtiness, and receive with meekness the engrafted word, which is able to save our souls"** (James 1:21).

It is obvious that the Psalmist understood this truth: **"It is good for me that I have been afflicted; that I might learn thy statutes"** (Psalms 119:71).

Scripture plainly teaches us that if we wish to be comforted, we must first mourn in repentance for our sin. There will be no raising up until there is first a laying down. Life can only spring out of death (John 12:24-25; 1 Corinthians 15:36).

The Holy Spirit tells us through the apostle Peter that there are four things that happen after we suffer a while in Christ: **"But the God of all grace, who hath called us unto his eternal glory by Christ Jesus, after that ye have suffered a while, make you <u>perfect</u>, <u>stablish</u>, <u>strengthen</u>, <u>settle</u> you"** (1 Peter 5:10).

Resurrection transformation in the form of maturing, solidification, grounding, strength, and joy come only, and **"after"** we mourn in our sufferings, choose repentance, and submit to the death of the self-life.

Mourning for Joy!

"Love is the key. Joy is love singing. Peace is love resting. Patience is love enduring. Kindness is love's truth. Goodness is love's character. Faithfulness is love's habit. Gentleness is love's self-forgetfulness." –Donald G. Barnhouse

We must be willing to **"mourn"** in order to experience divine comfort and joy. The seasons of sufferings are a blessing in that they assist in our death and burial which precedes Christ's resurrection life raising us upward (2 Corinthians 4:8-12). **"He that is dead is freed from sin"** (Romans 6:7). The disciple must be willing and obedient to do things God's way—to die in order to experience resurrection.

> **"If ye be willing and obedient, ye shall eat the good of the land: [20] But if ye refuse and rebel, ye shall be devoured with the sword: for the mouth of the LORD hath spoken it." Isaiah 1:19-20**

"Blessed are they that mourn: for they shall be comforted" (Matthew 5:4). The **"comfort"** of Christ's resurrection grace in our lives is utterly priceless. No matter what we may be walking through, His comfort will fill us as we remain rooted and grounded in the cross He prescribed (Luke 9:23-24).

As a disciple of Jesus, we're going to be persecuted and yet, we can take comfort in His comfort!

> *"I don't care who hates me. I care who loves me. Especially, when the One who loves me has power over the one who hates me."* –John Cameron

The words **"mourn"** and **"mourning"** appear 96 times in God's Word. Ever heard a message on it?

Regrettably, the biblical doctrine of mourning is nowhere to be found in the modern church, along with the doctrine of suffering. Why? Well, these truths don't entertain the goats which modern pastors have deceitfully corralled for their own self-serving purposes (Isaiah 30:9-10; Philippians 3:18-19; 2 Timothy 4:2-4).

> *"A church fed on excitement is no new testament church at all. The desire for surface stimulation is a sure mark of the fallen nature. The very thing Christ died to deliver us from."* –A.W. Tozer

Feast or Famine?

Have you noticed that most messages <u>in the apostate modern church</u>, center upon the feasting and never the mourning? Their assignment from Satan is to mislead, ultimately bringing damnation. Read closely the following treasure of a passage, noticing what is **"better"**:

> **"It is <u>better</u> to go to the house of mourning, than to go to the house of feasting: for that is the end of all men; and the living will lay**

it to his heart. [3] Sorrow is better than laughter: for by the sadness of the countenance the heart is made better. [4] The heart of the wise is in the house of mourning; but the heart of fools is in the house of mirth. [5] It is better to hear the rebuke of the wise, than for a man to hear the song of fools." Ecclesiastes 7:2-5

We all love to be at a celebration, right? Yet only those who sincerely know and walk with the LORD—on His stated terms—are granted by Him a clean heart of contrition and can therefore truly enjoy times of celebration.

Perhaps, when we begin to grasp this divine truth of being stripped, and cherish the outcome of it, we will begin welcoming times of mourning, trials, weeping, and repentance in returning to the LORD as our "**first love**" (Revelation 2:4-5).

"The blueness of a wound cleanseth away evil: so do stripes the inward parts of the belly." Proverbs 20:30

Remember when you were punished as a child? Remember how you cried in your room, reflecting on your offense? Then, remember how internally cleansed and well-adjusted you felt afterwards? **"Foolishness is bound in the heart of a child; but the rod of correction shall drive it far from him"** (Proverbs 22:15).

Regrettably, there are few who teach the cross today. Most preachers seek to keep you in the house or the realm of feasting instead of mourning for your sins. They coddle their prey in their sins, and most never teach what God's Word clearly states about holiness, walking in the holy fear of God, the daily cross, eagerly anticipating and preparing for the return of Christ, etc. They are preaching **"another gospel"** which is a false gospel and are **"accursed"** (Galatians 1:6-9). In doing this, those who patronize these church busine$$e$ are bogged down in their sins, unable to overcome, **"Ever learning, and never able to come to the knowledge of the truth"** (2 Timothy 3:7).

Overcoming the flesh, walking in victory, requires continually delighting in the LORD, worshipping Him **"in spirit and in truth"** (John 4:23-24).

God will never raise us up while we are still alive under our own power, doing our own thing, operating out of a self-serving agenda. Surrender. **"Therefore also now, saith the LORD, turn ye even to me**

with all your heart, and with fasting, and with weeping, and with mourning" (Joel 2:12).

Fasting is the obedience of self-inflicted mourning (death and burial), a putting to death of the self-life, in compliance with the stated divine mandate—the command of God to deny self, take up the cross, and follow Christ (Luke 9:23-24; Romans 6; Galatians 5:24). Resurrection will follow (2 Corinthians 4:10-12).

Some insist upon continual feasting or short-term comfort, celebration. Though celebration for specific things is the gift of God, *always* wanting to be celebrating seems to identify a deeper heart issue—a lack of understanding of the cross principle—where the saint dies downward, and God lifts Him upward.

Until we grasp and experience His cross in our daily lives, nothing is going to work as God intended. Here's the prayer of Jesus: **"Father, if thou be willing, remove this cup from me: nevertheless <u>not my will, but thine, be done</u>"** (Luke 22:42).

Are you willing to pray this prayer today? Are you willing to declare to the LORD **"not my will, but thine, be done"**?

Those who don't camp on this message of the cross but rather seek to circumvent it, will not experience the victory Christ died to procure for His beloved saints. It is only in bowing down low that God will lift His people high. This is the death, burial, and resurrection in our daily lives.

John the Baptist declared: **"He must increase, but I must decrease"** (John 3:30). Have you declared this today?

Though nearly never heard in the modern church, the message of the cross is the irreplaceable centerpiece of the original Gospel.

> **"I am crucified with Christ: nevertheless I live; yet not I, but Christ liveth in me: and the life which I now live in the flesh I live by the faith of the Son of God, who loved me, and gave himself for me." Galatians 2:20**

> **"Always bearing about in the body the dying of the Lord Jesus, that the life also of Jesus might be made manifest in our body. [11] For we which live are alway delivered unto death for Jesus' sake, that the life also of Jesus might be made manifest in our mortal flesh. [12] So then**

death worketh in us, but life in you." 2 Corinthians 4:10-12

"For ye are dead, and your life is hid with Christ in God." Colossians 3:3

PRAYER: *LORD, I am not my own, but now I am bought by the ultimate price of Your precious blood dear LORD Jesus. Right now, and from now forward LORD Jesus, You must increase but I must decrease. Sobeit. In the name of Jesus.*

Chapter 14

The Importance of Personal, Organic Bible Study

"Every word of God is pure: he is a shield *(protection)* **unto them that put their trust in him. [6] Add thou not unto his words, lest he reprove thee, and thou be found a liar." Proverbs 30:5-6**

Purity and authenticity are inseparable. **"Keep thyself pure"** (1 Timothy 5:22).

Divine discernment and inoculation from viral heretical infection comes from studying, knowing God's Word for yourself, organically!

"Blessed are the pure in heart: for they shall see God" (Matthew 5:8). To study the Bible, the pure words of God organically, means simply to study God's Word without the influence, the tainting of mere men! There is no other path to **"see God"** but to be **"pure in heart."**

God's Word is your life (Proverbs 4:20-23). The Word is your **"daily bread,"** and your life depends on knowing and obeying it (Matthew 6:11). Knowing and adhering to Holy Scripture is your protection (Proverbs 30:5-6).

We must obey the hunger and thirst the LORD gave us upon saving us for voraciously reading and studying His Word (1 Peter 2:2; 2 Timothy 2:15).

As disciples of Jesus, our mornings—every morning—begins in fellowship with Jesus and the Father, without exception!

In a very engaging fellowship discussion one morning with a dear brother in Christ, it was a blessing to witness his Berean approach to the LORD and His kingdom (Acts 17:10-11). He was factoring everything we discussed with Scripture, stopping to meditate and cite Holy Scripture. 2 Timothy 3:16-17 anyone? Amen Jesus!

God gave us His Word in written format so there would be no confusion, and no excuse on Judgment Day (John 12:48; Romans 2:16; 1 Corinthians 14:33; 2 Timothy 3:16-17, etc.). The Word of God is the basis by which the LORD shall judge each of us.

If in the endeavor of ministry, I've not gotten people into God's Word for themselves, I am an utter failure! God have mercy!

Organic Bible study, organic fellowship, and organic ministry simply refers to being "without foreign additives - poisons, tainting, pure." May Jesus bless His people with absolute authenticity.

So many among us are living wasted lives—lives that have been seduced into systems of theology, which contain poisons in the pond of their body of truth (the whole of what they believe).

Saints, let's beware of the charts and systems men create to "help people understand the Bible better." RED FLAG! God has ordered, commanded you to learn straight from Him and that's why you have access to His Word. You have a Bible. Study it for yourself. Your knowledge and understanding of God must of necessity come straight from your own personal, daily study of His Word. **"Study to shew thyself approved unto God, a workman that needeth not to be ashamed, rightly dividing the word of truth"** (2 Timothy 2:15). Antichrist cults in our midst that push the use of their charts and theological systems include the demonic dispensationalists, and many of the eschatology (end times) wolves.

We must obtain our theology, our knowledge of God, directly from the Word of God alone. We must learn of the LORD, learn for ourselves who the LORD is and what He said, and stop following man's philosophies, notions, systems, and charts. When the Bereans tested what Paul taught, they didn't break out some mere man's system, theology, or a chart. No, they **"searched the scriptures daily"** to see if Paul was preaching the truth (Acts 17:10-11).

Many a believer has been misled by the teachings, the charts, and systems of evil men posing as Christ's elders. Run from them! Stop and think: *"Why would those men build a system, a theology, a chart for you to follow instead of exhorting you to study the topic in God's Word for yourself—just as God commanded you to do?"* The only reason why wolves create systems and charts is to get you to believe their errors and to derail gullible people who refuse to study God's Word for themselves (2 Timothy 2:15).

If a man isn't in the Word, learning the Word and meditating on the Word, he has no business acting as if he's ministering for Christ! Such a man's knowledge of God is second hand at best. Today is the day to return to the LORD and to get in His Word with reckless abandonment! Get lost in it and it will then and only then get into you! (2 Timothy 2:15)

After confronting a lady (who was being misled by dispensational wolves), exhorting her to study God's Word organically for herself instead of via wolves, she said:

> *"We can't claim the whole Bible to ourselves. We don't all have to go out and build arks ... Paul's epistles are different for a reason as with Hebrews."*

The reply given:

> *"You are using mere human reasoning. The Holy Spirit and the Holy Scriptures are our Teachers, not mere men. Paul told Timothy to study the Word of God for himself (2 Timothy 2:15). Yes, we as Christ's true body, are to dwell richly in God's Word and yet, regrettably, you've been misled by an enemy of Christ, a false teacher, who is not of the body of Christ but rather one of the wolves Jesus and His apostles so often warned us about (Acts 2:42; Colossians 3:17, etc.)."*

Contrary to the apostles of Jesus, most ministries and ministers today intentionally foster in their target market, their prey, a dependence upon them and not Christ. They want to entice and seduce in order to create a following, a repeat customer base, and build their church or ministry busine$$. Beware saints.

Are you **"Taught of God"** or are you taught of man? See John 6:45; 1 Thessalonians 4:9.

> **"Wherefore the Lord said, Forasmuch as this people draw near me with their mouth, and with their lips do honour me, but have removed their heart far from me, and their fear toward me is <u>taught by the precept of men</u>:" Isaiah 29:13**

Those not diligently, daily in God's Word for themselves are sitting ducks for a deceiver to come along in their vacuum and fill the void with heresy. It will very likely happen if it hasn't already. Beloved of God, if you wish to endure to the end, you must personally fill your heart and mind with God's Word or you will be turned over to **"strong delusion"** (2 Thessalonians 2:9-12). God takes it personally when a person chooses not to love His truth!

> **"Study to shew thyself approved unto God, a workman that needeth not to be ashamed, rightly dividing the word of truth." 2 Timothy 2:15**

The individual nature of this instruction is introduced at the onset of this verse: **"Study to shew <u>thyself</u> approved unto God."** *You* do it.

Yet, instead of personally studying the Bible organically, some want a short cut and so they become snared in the net of some ministry that is pushing a system, pretending to make it easier for them to understand the Bible. Laziness is also a contributing factor when men choose to go to seminary—to supposedly study a book they've had in their possession for their whole life. At seminary they pay big bucks for someone else to tell them what it says instead of simply reading it for themselves. At seminary they are enlisting and paying to be indoctrinated.

Saints of Christ, be aware that clever men, operating as Christian pastors, authors, singers, etc., can make nearly anything look biblical. They perform this sleight of hand, this trickery by selectively siphoning out Bible verses to make their point, to make their heresy or heretical tradition look legit. Yet they do this to the exclusion of the whole of Scripture, which they hope you never thoroughly study.

These are the very wolves in sheep's clothing we've been warned about. They take advantage of the ignorance of their prey (Hosea 4:6). We must test the spirits by asking whether or not their doctrine is expressly, directly, explicitly stated in the whole of Holy Scripture, or not—just exactly as the Berean disciples did when Paul came preaching (Acts 17:10-11; 1 John 4:1).

Again, nearly anything can be extrapolated and supposedly "proven" using select Scriptures and yet, is that what the whole of Scripture communicates? Test. Discern. Beware of the sleight of hand manipulators who only visit, quote, and acknowledge the parts of the Bible they wish in order to manipulate their audience. **"Beloved, believe not every spirit, but try the spirits whether they are of God: because many false prophets are gone out into the world"** (1 John 4:1).

Today, the *true* body of Christ, is **"Looking unto Jesus"** and not mere men (Hebrews 12:1-3). **"Knowing that of the Lord ye shall receive the reward of the inheritance: for ye serve the Lord Christ"** (Colossians 3:24).

You are not dependent upon mere men, ministers or ministries, but upon the LORD your God and Savior—Jesus!

"Ye are bought with a price; be not ye the servants of men." 1 Corinthians 7:23

One of the great deceptions in today's "church" is that many "pastors" verbally claim that God's Word is the highest authority, then they cling to something that contradicts God's Word. When confronted they ditch the Word of God for their tradition, their heresy or doctrine of men. This is exactly what Jesus cited the false leaders of His day for doing (Mark 7:6-9, 13).

Many wish to be bonded to hell, to lies, to falsehood. They cling to their heretical traditions, setting aside the very Word of God to do so (Mark 7:6-9).

> **"Because ye have said, We have made a covenant with death, and with hell are we at agreement; when the overflowing scourge shall pass through, it shall not come unto us: for <u>we have made lies our refuge, and under falsehood have we hid ourselves</u>:" Isaiah 28:15**

The Fear of God

One example of this manipulating and isolating of Scripture is the sacred cow, golden calf doctrine of eternal security otherwise called once saved always saved. Any person who believes the demonic heresy of unconditional eternal security, will not fear God, **"There is no fear of God before their eyes"** (Romans 3:18), or take sin seriously as God does, who is **"Holy, holy, holy"** (Isaiah 6:3; Revelation 4:8).

To be turned from **"the snares of death"** one must fear the LORD. **"The fear of the LORD is a fountain of life, to depart from the snares of death"** (Proverbs 14:27).

Praying in the name of Jesus to the Father, asking Him to help you never be misled, is vital. **"Seek ye out of the book of the LORD, and read: no one of these shall fail"** (Isaiah 34:16).

Many today would rather find someone to tell them what the Bible says instead of studying it for themselves. Deadly mistake. Hell is full of people who did this—instead of seeking the LORD fervently, daily, diligently for themselves as He instructed us to do (2 Timothy 2:15).

If a person isn't in the Word, learning the Word and meditating on the Word, he has no business acting as if he is ministering for Christ! Such a person's knowledge of God is second hand at best. Wisdom would be to repent now and get into God's Word with reckless abandonment! When we get into the Word it will then and only then get into us! See 2 Timothy 2:15.

Friend, if you don't personally diligently study God's written Word for yourself, you will forfeit a myriad of divine blessings and will be deceived—and in the end **"destroyed"** (2 Thessalonians 2:9-12; Hosea 4:6; Matthew 22:29; 2 Timothy 2:15; 3:16-17).

> **"All scripture is given by inspiration of God, and is profitable for doctrine, for reproof, for correction, for instruction in righteousness: [17] that the man of God may be perfect, throughly furnished unto all good works." 2 Timothy 3:16-17**

The less involvement of man, the better. Studying the Bible organically is the best method, thoroughly, topically, stacking Scripture upon Scripture. **"For precept must be upon precept, precept upon**

precept; line upon line, line upon line; here a little, and there a little" (Isaiah 28:10).

Scripture teaches us how to decipher truth in 1 Corinthians 2:13: "**Which things also we speak, not in the words which man's wisdom teacheth, but which the Holy Ghost teacheth; comparing spiritual things with spiritual"** (1 Corinthians 2:13).

The Bible is its own built-in dictionary. Dictionary definitions can also help at times and yet should be taken in measure, into consideration, and not to be fully relied upon. The goal is to prayerfully and through diligent, thorough study of the whole of God's Word, see what is being conveyed. It is this author's experience and opinion that *Webster's American 1828 Dictionary* is the best.

What happens in most apostate modern churches is indoctrination—not true Bible learning. People are being poisoned by the doctrines of men and devils.

You have a Bible? Good. Read it for yourself (2 Timothy 2:15). Let's stop relying on mere men to teach us what only the Scriptures and the Holy Spirit who gave them can teach us.

The LORD who bought you with His blood wants you to be taught of Him and the only way that can rightly happens is if you make His Word your final authority and live like it by studying it daily (2 Timothy 2:15).

Let the Bible speak for itself. If someone is trying to convince you that the Bible says something instead of letting God speak for Himself—letting His Word speak to you—that should be a red flag. There are lots of voices saying, *"the Bible says,"* and yet until you personally behold it with your own eyes in God's Word, you should not embrace it. **"In the mouth of two or three witnesses shall every word be established"** (2 Corinthians 13:1).

We as men can find Scripture to justify nearly anything. Men can deceitfully extrapolate and "prove" nearly anything using the right mixture of Scripture taken out of the context of what the whole of Scripture teaches.

Attention: It's okay for all of us to humble ourselves and be teachable. We all have lots to learn (Proverbs 1:5; 15:32).

The Bible Instructs Us How to Interpret the Bible

No Greek or Hebrew is needed and is certainly not the main rule of interpretation. We must take God's preserved Word for what it clearly states in our own language, as we thoroughly compile, compound, put together and compare Scripture with Scripture (Isaiah 28:16; 1 Corinthians 2:13). This is the biblically revealed method of priority in apprehending truth, the highest stated rule of interpreting truth. A thorough gathering of all Scripture pertaining to the given topic is essential.

Just because someone's book, a website, or some man standing in a pulpit says something, in no way makes it true. You must **"prove *(test)* all things"** and only hold fast the truth. **"Prove all things; hold fast that which is good"** (1 Thessalonians 5:21).

> **"And the brethren immediately sent away Paul and Silas by night unto Berea: who coming thither went into the synagogue of the Jews. [11] <u>These were more noble than those in Thessalonica, in that they received the word with all readiness of mind, and</u>**

searched the scriptures daily, whether those things were so." Acts 17:10-11

God gave you His Word, so you'd trust *Him*, not men or ministries: "**That your faith should not stand in the wisdom of men, but in the power of God"** (1 Corinthians 2:5).

PRAYER: *LORD, I want to ask You to circumcise my heart, to cut away all deceit which I here and now denounce. Please grant my heart a deep desire to learn the whole of Your Word, to be thorough, honest, and comprehensive in the study of Your bless-ed precepts. In Jesus' Name.*

Chapter 15

Authentically Honest

"For I will declare mine iniquity; I will be sorry for my sin." Psalms 38:18

We must always CONFESS and not COVER our sins. Think: Honesty.

Authentic followers of Jesus do not make excuses for sin. No, they immediately go to Christ in repentance, receive His merciful forgiveness and lay down their lives before Him, afresh.

Like David, who cried out to God in repentance after he had sinned, each of us has more than abundant reason to cry out to God! Read Psalms 51.

The man after God's own heart readily admitted and confessed his sins. He didn't cover them because David chose to be honest before the LORD. He also understood that the LORD sees all, and nothing can be hidden from Him. You would do well today friend to declare these very words encased in Scripture as did the beloved David: **"For I will declare mine iniquity; I will be sorry for my sin"** (Psalms 38:18).

> **"I acknowledged my sin unto thee, and mine iniquity have I not hid. I said, I will confess my transgressions unto the LORD; and thou forgavest the iniquity of my sin. Selah. 6 For this shall every one that is godly pray unto thee in a time when thou mayest be found** *(before it's too late)***: surely in the floods of great waters they shall not come nigh unto him." Psalms 32:5-6**

Departing from all iniquity must begin with divine conviction and may God bless us to become transparent with Him—authentic, pure, honest.

> **"Nevertheless the foundation of God standeth sure, having this seal, The Lord knoweth them that are his. And, Let <u>every one</u> that nameth the name of Christ depart from iniquity." 2 Timothy 2:19**

Departing from iniquity is the divine command for "**<u>every one</u> that nameth the name of Christ."** We must never make excuse to for sin nor seek to cover it.

Jesus cited two chosen qualities of those who will be with Him eternally: **"But that on the good ground are they, which in an <u>honest</u> and <u>good</u>**

heart, having heard the word, keep it, and bring forth fruit with patience" (Luke 8:15).

Choosing to worship, to serve the LORD **"in an honest and good heart"** is essential to eternal glory.

We cannot get free until we get honest.

> **"Now is the judgment of this world: now shall the prince of this world be cast out. [32] And I, if I be lifted up from the earth, will draw all men unto me. [33] This he said, signifying what death he should die." John 12:31-33**

Jesus judged sin on the cross, so we don't have to be judged for our sin, if we admit, repent, and confess (Proverbs 28:13; 1 John 1:9, etc.).

The claims of the Father's justice to redeem mankind could only and exclusively have been satisfied by the perfect sacrifice of His only begotten Son (2 Corinthians 5:19). On the sole basis of the perfection of the LORD Jesus, the Lamb of God who shed His blood on that cross for our sins, lies our redemption.

Until the reality of how sinful, how hopeless, how depraved we are compared to the matchless holiness of God begins to set in, we are unable to begin to appreciate the grand blessings of the redemption of Christ. You may wish to pause and pray for this realization beloved.

A good beginning toward authenticity would include honest confession, acknowledging before God that you are worthy of nothing but destruction and damnation and that without Christ's perfect sacrifice, you are doomed. Thanksgiving for His **"unspeakable gift,"** which is Christ, is in order *daily* for each of us (2 Corinthians 9:15).

Seems like it's fallen human nature to hide in our sin, our iniquitous leanings, instead of simply stopping and asking the LORD, praying something like: *Heavenly Father, would You please change me from the inside out concerning this matter of ________________? Please do a deep work in my heart dear Father in the name of Jesus Christ. Amen.*

Saved by Divine Mercy

> **"When he had by himself purged our sins, sat down on the right hand of the Majesty on high." Hebrews 1:3**

Our salvation was earned, merited by Christ alone, not ourselves. **"But we are all as an unclean thing, and all our righteousnesses are as filthy rags…"** (Isaiah 64:6).

> **"Not by works of righteousness which we have done, but according to his mercy he saved us, by the washing of regeneration, and renewing of the Holy Ghost; [6] Which he shed on us abundantly through Jesus Christ our Saviour; [7] That being justified by his grace, we should be made heirs according to the hope of eternal life." Titus 3:5-7**

Do we still think we were worthy to be forgiven and saved? …. Not! God did it out of His sheer love! Can we examine that idea?

> **"As it is written, There is none righteous, no, not one:" Romans 3:10**

"I am not worthy of the least of all the mercies, and of all the truth, which thou hast shewed unto thy servant." Genesis 32:10

"For I know that in me (that is, in my flesh,) dwelleth no good thing: for to will is present with me; but how to perform that which is good I find not." Romans 7:18

The truth makes no one free until they repent, embrace, and obey it (John 8:31-32).

Once you repent (re-turn) to the LORD and confess your sins, OTHER than blasphemy of the Holy Ghost, what sin is there that you or anyone else committed that is unforgiveable? None! We can go to the throne of His grace **"that we may obtain mercy and find grace, to help in time of need."** In Christ, at His throne of grace, not judgment, we receive these gifts (Hebrews 4:14-16). As a result of His mercy and grace received, we can let it all go, be cleansed all the way to the core of our conscience and press forward (Philippians 3:13-14; Hebrews 9:14; 1 John 1:9, etc.).

Divine Mercy by the Blood of the Lamb!

"He hath not dealt with us after our sins; nor rewarded us according to our iniquities.[11] For as the heaven is high above the earth, so great is his mercy toward them that fear him. [12] As far as the east is from the west, so far hath he removed our transgressions from us." Psalms 103:10-12

There are two types of professing Christians:

1. Heaven-bound: Those who have been born again and abide in Christ. They face the LORD honestly in true repentance with their own utter depravity and sin, fasting and prayer, the cross (crucified), fighting the good fight of faith in a grounded, daily walk with Jesus, and then there are ...

2. Those who choose to be dishonest and deceitful of heart, unrepentant, walking in and loving darkness rather than light, and so these migrate to false teachers and false teachings to justify their sins. They attempt to hide from personal accountability for their sins, dismissing all personal responsibility before

> God. They cover instead of confessing their sins to their own destruction. Out of the image of their own wicked hearts these apostates make to themselves gods of the false teachers and their sin-justifying teachings (2 Timothy 4:2-4). This is the whole Satanic construct and system of Calvinism, eternal security/OSAS and the hiding place for moral cowards who refuse to present themselves honestly before the LORD in repentance and confession of sin (Proverbs 28:13; John 3:19-21; James 4:6-10).

Jesus requires that we simply come to Him in an **"honest and good heart"** (Luke 8:15). He beckons us to cry out to Him in sincere humility and repentance–just as did one of the two men of whom Jesus spoke who went up to pray. The one whose prayer was heard by God simply prayed: **"God be merciful to me a sinner"** (Luke 18:13).

> **"I acknowledged my sin unto thee and mine iniquity have I not hid. I said, I will confess my transgressions unto the LORD; and thou forgavest the iniquity of my sin. Selah." Psalms 32:5**

Being knowledgeable about God is separate from being honest with God, which is an act of the heart and will. Only **"honest"** souls will be in Heaven. Pride prevents honesty and is soul damning (Proverbs 16:18; 18:12). When a man won't humble himself, he will cover his sins, and refuse to openly acknowledge them before God (Psalms 32:5; 38:18; Proverbs 28:13; Luke 8:15; James 4:6-10; 1 John 1:9, etc.).

Who are Jesus' authentic followers? Have you memorized this Bible verse yet? **"He that <u>covereth</u>** *(hides)* **his sins shall not prosper: but whoso confesseth and forsaketh them shall have mercy"** (Proverbs 28:13).

Want to see an authentic truth-seeker? They are honest about their own utter, desperate need for Jesus today! (Read Psalms 51; 32:5; 38:18; 69:5; Matthew 5:3; Luke 18:13.) They are fighting the good fight of faith and do not make excuse for their sin but rather confess and forsake it, cutting off the hand and plucking out the eye—whatever it takes (Proverbs 28:13; Mark 9:43-49; 1 Timothy 6:12).

God is presently working in their lives, unlike the self-serving OSAS counterfeits who choose to hide behind a myth and have a mere **"form of**

godliness" and from whom the LORD has departed (Philippians 2:12-13; 2 Timothy 3:5).

Let this be stated again, that like David, each of us has more than abundant reason to cry out to God! Read Psalms 51.

When a man gets honest with God, he will no longer migrate to false teaching to excuse, deny, defend, or justify his sin. Instead, he will prayerfully seek out true disciples who are known by their adherence to Holy Scripture (John 8:47).

Those who vainly believe the OSAS mythology want to stop at Jesus' cross. This tribe of counterfeits wants nothing to do with personal responsibility and the crucified life Jesus mandates in order to follow Him now, and to be with Him for eternity in glory. In fact, they brand anyone who communicates BIBLE truth that speaks of these things as teaching works-based salvation (Luke 9:23-24). Hell awaits. **"So likewise, whosoever he be of you that forsaketh not all that he hath, he cannot be my disciple"** (Luke 14:33).

When a person believes OSAS/eternal security, it clearly reveals that:

1. They are not being honest with God (Luke 8:15).

2. They are not honest with His Word (Romans 3:4).

3. They are self-deceived and following false teaching (Titus 3:10-11).

4. Perhaps God has sent them a **"strong delusion"** because they didn't receive the love of His truth (2 Thessalonians 2:9-12).

5. They are not studying to show their own selves approved to God but rather following snakes who tell them what their unrepentant hearts want to hear—tickle their ears (2 Timothy 2:15; 4:2-5; Jude 3-4; Isaiah 30:9-10, etc.).

6. They have forgotten that God is holy and have turned the grace of God into "lasciviousness" — a license to sin (Jude 3-4).

7. They are no longer saved by grace because they continue in sin instead of repenting, confessing their sin, and obeying God (Romans 6:1-2; 11:20-22, etc.).

8. They are in danger of hell fire and it's going to be worse than if they'd never known, experienced initial salvation (Ezekiel 33:12-13; 2 Peter 2:20-21).

9. Like Adam and Eve who bought this same lie, they have departed from the faith due to **"giving heed to seducing spirits and doctrines of devils"** (1 Timothy 4:1-2; Genesis 2:17; 3:4).

10. They didn't endure to the end through trying times and fell away even though they still have a **"form of godliness"** (Luke 8:13; 2 Timothy 3:5).

Jesus requires utter honesty, true repentance, good fruit to prove it, and that you endure to the end to be saved into eternal glory (Matthew 3:7-10; 10:22; 24:13; Luke 8:15; 13:3, etc.). Being an authentic disciple of Jesus is a relationship. Will you be like the five wise or five foolish virgins? Will you be in the eternal bridal chamber with the heavenly Bridegroom, or will you be shut out of it for choosing to fall out of intimate fellowship with Him leading up to the wedding day? (Read Matthew 25:1-13.)

PRAYER: *Holy Father, I come to You now on the basis of Christ and His perfect sacrifice on that cross for me, for my sins. LORD, please affect me with Your holy fear and holiness at the very core of my being. Make my heart, my spirit, to be fully transparent, utterly honest with You concerning all things, and extremely sensitive to Your impressions, convictions, rebukes, and leading. Please break me LORD and make me of a humble and contrite spirit who trembles at your Word. And please make me one with You. Please fill me with Your Holy Spirit afresh and use me! In the name of Jesus Christ, amen.*

[illegible]

Chapter 16

Authentic Evangelism

"Now then we are ambassadors for Christ, as though God did beseech you by us we pray you in Christ's stead, be ye reconciled to God." 2 Corinthians 5:20

The LORD calls His true disciples as **"ambassadors for Christ,"** and as such to represent Christ, not self. Self must be set aside, crucified out of the way, and Christ must reign—the life of the cross (Galatians 2:20).

> **"For we preach not ourselves, but Christ Jesus the Lord; and ourselves your servants for Jesus' sake." 2 Corinthians 4:5**
>
> **"For I determined not to know any thing among you, save Jesus Christ, and him crucified." 1 Corinthians 2:2**

As the great apostle **"determined"** to **"know"** and represent Christ alone, **"ambassadors"** do not serve themselves but rather those whom they are sent by. They function on the behalf of their sender. In the case of believers, we are envoys representing **"an holy nation"** that is not of this world and as such we are in need of our King's unction (1 Peter 2:9).

As a diplomat for a country for example, the envoy must meet a certain, high standard of behavior which involves representing his country and if not, history tells us that he will fall into disrepute for not fulfilling his duties.

An ambassador has mandates to fulfill and therefore must be diligent to accomplish those directives with integrity.

As a representative for a country one must stay free from entanglements that would hinder him from accomplishing his duties, so must the ambassador for Christ.

Note here that the victory of Christ appropriated in our lives involves making us free to be **"always abounding in the work of the Lord."** Friend, are you involved in the **"work of the Lord"**?

> **"But thanks be to God, which giveth us the victory through our Lord Jesus Christ.**
> **58 Therefore, my beloved brethren, be ye**

stedfast, unmoveable, always abounding in the work of the Lord, forasmuch as ye know that your labour is not in vain in the Lord." 1 Corinthians 15:57-58

Each and every believer should be personally involved in **"the work of the Lord,"** and **"the work of the Lord"** must be done the LORD's way, and no other way.

As authentic followers of Jesus, we must communicate the words of God and not our own. We must do things God's way, not our way.

"They that sow in tears shall reap in joy. [6] He that goeth forth and weepeth, bearing precious seed, shall doubtless come again with rejoicing, bringing his sheaves *(harvest)* **with him." Psalms 126:5-6**

A harvest of blessed souls is going to be the result, the ministry harvest, the fruit of all who bear and scatter the seed of the incorruptible Word of God into the hearts of men (1 Peter 1:23).

God didn't say, *"Go explain who I am to other people."* No, He said, **"preach the word"** and **"preach the gospel"** (2 Timothy 4:2; Mark 16:15).

We still have the tendency to be wise in our **"own conceits"** (Romans 12:16). May the LORD bless us with true repentance, resulting in allowing God to speak for Himself by simply giving people His Word in His love and wisdom (Colossians 3:16; 2 Timothy 4:2, etc.).

The Word of God must become the primary emphasis and not us, not our finite wonderful, skillful explanations.

> **"Being born again, not of corruptible seed, but of incorruptible, by the word of God, which liveth and abideth for ever. [24] For all flesh is as grass, and all the glory of man as the flower of grass. The grass withereth, and the flower thereof falleth away: [25] But the word of the Lord endureth for ever. And this is the word which by the gospel is preached unto you." 1 Peter 1:23-25**

The incorruptible seed is the Word of God and not just our *explanation* of Him. People are born again by the incorruptible seed of the Word itself and not our explanation.

Dale Wren writes: *"And we are not called to dialogue, but to earnestly contend for the faith once delivered to the saints."*

This is so true. Other than on Mars Hill (Acts 17) where Paul simply pointed the searchers to the one true God, most of what we see in Christ and His apostles' ministries is teaching and preaching the Word, the truth (Matthew 28:18-20; Mark 16:15).

Today, many ministries are formed which endlessly dialogue with people, lost people (such as so-called "atheists") in order to somehow convince them to become a Christian—as if they can be talked into regeneration. Ravi Zacharias is one example of how a man can philosophize about the existence of God without ever using Scripture—when God's Word is the only way people will be convicted and saved into Christ's kingdom. Yet millions of professing Christians patronized, supported, and follow these types of Bible-less, Scripture-less "ministries." **"The law of the LORD is perfect, converting the soul: the testimony of the LORD is sure, making wise the simple"** (Psalms 19:7).

As is observed in the New Testament, dialoguing with sinners is not how God works to save souls, that's not primarily how people are saved into Christ's kingdom. When God saves someone, it's usually when the Word is taught or especially preached, and the lost souls repent and are saved due to their conviction of being in the state of sin, separated from their Maker and hell bound.

Think the Day of Pentecost when Peter preached and 3,000 souls were saved, then 5,000 (Acts 2-4). Also, the testimony of the saints leads to others being saved such as the woman at the well who testified of Christ and many began following Jesus (John 4). See Revelation 12:11.

God's Word Spoken, Accomplishes His Will

> **"So shall my word be that goeth forth out of my mouth: it shall not return unto me void, but it shall accomplish that which I please, and it shall prosper in the thing whereto I sent it." Isaiah 55:11**

It is the Word that never returns to God void, not our explanation.

When you encounter a person in darkness and they act contrary, don't take it personally. No, rather, see it as an opportunity to kindly plant the seed of the Word of God in their heart—which never returns to the LORD void but always accomplishes that which pleases him (Isaiah 55:11). **"God is love"** (1 John 4:8, 16).

The emphasis should not be on our ability to explain God but rather on His Word and simply obeying him by preaching it. It's the incorruptible seed, God's Word that brings conviction and salvation, not our words (1 Peter 1:23).

> **"Study to shew thyself approved unto God, a workman that needeth not to be ashamed, rightly dividing the word of truth." 2 Timothy 2:15**

Regrettably, lots of people brag about their pastor and how he (supposedly) preaches the Word. In most cases it's obvious that they're telegraphing that they trust the mere man, the pastor, are enamored with him, and have no life, no intimate relationship with Christ for themselves. The LORD desires that we know Him personally and this includes at the foundation, to be in His Word daily for ourselves—learning of Him (Matthew 11:28-30; John 17:3; 2 Timothy 2:15).

Hell is full of people who took men at their word instead of loving God enough to find out what He said in HIS Word for themselves, firsthand. Sad. If a man doesn't love God enough to prayerfully search out and pour over His words, His instructions, His promises, and His doctrines and warnings for himself, he is in utter need of true repentance and to seek the holy face of the LORD continually (1 Chronicles 16:11).

> **"But evil men and seducers shall wax worse and worse, deceiving, and being deceived. [14] But continue thou in the things which thou hast learned and hast been assured of, knowing of whom thou hast learned them; [15] <u>And that from a child thou hast known the holy scriptures, which are able to make thee wise unto salvation through faith which is in Christ Jesus</u>. [16] All scripture is given by inspiration of God, and is profitable for doctrine, for reproof, for correction, for instruction in righteousness: [17] That the man of God may be perfect, throughly furnished unto all good works." 2 Timothy 3:13-17**

Preach the Word

**"I charge thee therefore before God, and
the Lord Jesus Christ, who shall judge the
quick and the dead at his appearing and his
kingdom; 2 Preach the word; be instant in
season, out of season; reprove, rebuke,
exhort with all longsuffering and doctrine. 3
For the time will come when they will not
endure sound doctrine; but after their own
lusts shall they heap to themselves teachers,
having itching ears; 4 And they shall turn
away their ears from the truth, and shall be
turned unto fables." 2 Timothy 4:1-4**

The Parable of the Seed Growing

**"And he said, So is the kingdom of God, as if
a man should cast seed into the ground; 27
And should sleep, and rise night and day, and
the seed should spring and grow up, he
knoweth not how. 28 For the earth bringeth
forth fruit of herself; first the blade, then the
ear, after that the full corn in the ear. 29 But
when the fruit is brought forth, immediately
he putteth in the sickle, because the harvest
is come." Mark 4:26-29**

Conformed to Christ and therefore Full of His Compassion

Properly delivering the Good News, the Gospel of our LORD, requires that we are possessed with His view of the lost.

> **"But when he saw the multitudes, he was moved with compassion on them, because they fainted, and were scattered abroad, as sheep having no shepherd." Matthew 9:36**

With the goal of bringing us into the place of being an effective minister of Christ, our LORD and great Potter, will allow us to be stripped of all self-righteousness and full of the compassion and mercy of Christ (Matthew 9:35-38). This will require our personal participation in seeking God to be broken, purged, and cleansed of all that does not come from Christ, all self-righteousness and merciless unwarranted scorn of those in need of Christ—whether backslidden or the rank heathen who needs divine forgiveness. **"For the wrath of man worketh not the righteousness of God"** (James 1:20).

"For the wrath of God is revealed from heaven against all ungodliness and unrighteousness of men, who hold the truth in unrighteousness;" Romans 1:18

"And thinkest thou this, O man, that
judgest them which do such things, and
doest the same, that thou shalt escape the
judgment of God? 4 Or despisest thou the
riches of his goodness and forbearance and
longsuffering; not knowing that the
goodness of God leadeth thee to
repentance? 5 But after thy hardness and
impenitent heart treasurest up unto
thyself wrath against the day of wrath and
revelation of the righteous judgment of
God; 6 Who will render to every man
according to his deeds: 7 To them who by
patient continuance in well doing seek for
glory and honour and immortality, eternal
life: 8 But unto them that are contentious,
and do not obey the truth, but obey
unrighteousness, indignation and wrath, 9
Tribulation and anguish, upon every soul
of man that doeth evil, of the Jew first, and
also of the Gentile; 10 But glory, honour,
and peace, to every man that worketh good,
to the Jew first, and also to the Gentile: 11

For there is no respect of persons with God." Romans 2:3-11

Whenever you are speaking the words of God, you are preaching the judgment of GOD, not the judgment of mere men. **"Judge not according to the appearance, but judge righteous judgment"** (John 7:24). The words of God ARE specifically called the **"judgments"** of God. In Psalms 119 alone, the words of the LORD are called **"judgments"** 18 times. Inherent in His words are His **"judgments."**

While going about the business of preaching the Gospel I've had the experience of running into many sinners who recklessly judge others. So, along with giving them Jesus' words of warning in Matthew 7:1-5, here's my reply to one of them:

> *"God says (sinner's name) is a liar, thief, adulterer, fornicator, and you're guilty of committing every other sin under the sun. We've ALL sinned and are going to pay eternally for those sins in hell unless we repent and receive Jesus for the forgiveness of our sins. So, judging others is merely a smokescreen. You are 100 percent guilty of sin and in big trouble. Repent and receive Jesus before it's too late. God's Word*

says that you are going to hell if you don't repent and receive Christ."

The authentic disciple must cry out to the LORD to be stripped of every trace of iniquity that does not please Jesus Christ. Self-righteousness is one of those defiling attitudes. Personally, I've incorporated this following passage to daily recite and meditate on in order to dispel this evil of self-righteousness.

> **"Not by works of righteousness which we have done, but according to his mercy he saved us, by the washing of regeneration, and renewing of the Holy Ghost; 6 Which he shed on us abundantly through Jesus Christ our Saviour; 7 That being justified by his grace, we should be made heirs according to the hope of eternal life." Titus 3:5-7**

In short, all of Scripture testifies that God can and will use His honest, pure hearted disciples (Matthew 5:8; 2 Timothy 2:21, etc.).

Getting in on the Gospel action begins with a simple prayer, perhaps something like this ....

PRAYER: *LORD, please cleanse, prepare, and use me for Your glory. Here I am, please send me dear LORD. In Jesus' Name, amen.*

Making Peace with God

Are you ready to pass from death to life? The most astounding event of human history occurred when this man, Jesus Christ, died on a Roman cross. When He died, an untimely darkness covered the land at 3:00 p.m. and an earthquake occurred as He took His final breath. This man called Jesus was crucified. Three days later He was raised from the dead! Here's why He died:

"But your iniquities (sins) **have separated between you and your God, and your sins have hid his face from you, that he will not hear." ~ Isaiah 59:2**

God is holy, and our sins separate us from Him. We have all broken God's laws by lying, dishonoring our parents, cheating, hating, committing a sex act (even in our mind) with someone we are not married to, stealing, coveting, taking His holy name in vain, etc. These are all sins against God, and we are all guilty. Committing any single one of these sins makes us guilty of breaking the whole law and worthy of death.

Divine justice demands that our violations be punished. Because we are guilty of breaking God's holy law, we deserve to be fairly repaid for our offenses. God doesn't want us to be punished in hell forever though, so He sent His Son to pay the debt for us, so we would not have to pay for our own sins in eternal hell as we clearly deserve, but rather live now and forever with Him. What love!

At the end of a perfect (sinless) life, Christ carried the very cross He was to be nailed to. His infinite love for you, along with the nails driven through His hands and feet, held Him to that cross as He agonized for 6 hours in pain—to pay for your sins. He was crucified to make peace between God and man. The Son of God bridged the gap that sin had caused. This wonderful man named Jesus chose to shed His life blood (die—in excruciating pain) for you rather than live without you. He loves you.

"For the wages of sin is death; but the gift of God is eternal life through Jesus Christ our Lord." ~ Romans 6:23

Christ died to fully pay for the sins of the human race (John 19:30). God loves us and wants us to experience relationship with Him, now and forever (John 17:3). Friend, who else has ever died for you but Jesus, the Good Shepherd?

"For when we were yet without strength, in due time Christ died for the ungodly (that's you)**." ~ Romans 5:6**

Jesus Christ bears those scars in His holy hands and feet which prove how much He loves you (Romans 5:6-9; 2 Corinthians 5:19-21; 1 John 3:16). No one else ever died for your sins on a cruel cross—to buy you back to Himself. He **"gave himself a ransom for all, to be testified in due time" ~** (1 Timothy 2:6).

"Christ Jesus came into the world to save (rescue) **sinners." ~ 1 Timothy 1:15**

No religion or religious figure can save your soul from hell (no matter what they claim). Jesus didn't come to start a religion but rather to establish His eternal kingdom in the hearts of men, granting them a relationship with God. Jesus Christ is the only One who bears nail-scarred hands and feet for your sins. He is the only way to God and your only hope.

"For there is ONE God, and ONE mediator between God and men, the man Christ Jesus." ~ 1 Timothy 2:5

The Son of God died and rose again to take away all your sins. He was the only One qualified for the job and He is the only One worthy of your worship.

Peace with God Happens When We Meet the Prince of Peace.

It is by no accident you are reading this message. This is your moment in history to be saved. Praying and doing good deeds and going to church will save no person from eternal punishment. **"For by grace** (undeserved favor) **are ye saved through faith; and that not of yourselves: it is the gift of God: Not of works, lest any man should boast"** (Ephesians 2:8-9). Only the good work of Christ shedding His sinless blood on the cross for you will save your soul as you repent before a holy and righteous God and Judge.

If you are going to get right with the LORD and go to Heaven, there must be a moment of reckoning. Now is your time to be saved. No one will ever through a life of good works earn God's favor. There must, of necessity, be that divinely defining moment when you lay your whole life/being/existence into His perfect, holy hands.

Apply His holy blood to your life so that you may be saved, forgiven, and live eternally with Him. You must completely turn your life over to Him in repentance and faith.

In a moment of sincere solitude, get alone with God or pray with another true born-again Christian. Take yourself away from all else to honor the One who made you, bowing your heart to speak in prayer with Him who is Your God and Judge. He is listening. In fact, He's the very One who orchestrated all of this and brought you to this place.

Below is a model prayer. If you will pray to God sincerely and from the depths of your heart, in sincere repentance, turning to the LORD with all that is in you, the LORD will hear and answer your prayer and save you, washing away your sins in His blood.

Your Prayer of Repentance to God to be Saved

Dear heavenly Father, right now, if never before, I come to you as a broken and sinful person. Thank You for sending Your only begotten Son to die in my place for my sins. Thank You Jesus for coming to this earth to die and rise again to rescue me from sin and eternal hell and to save me for Your eternal glory. Right this moment, if never before, I receive You LORD Jesus. Come in and take over my whole life. I am all Yours and You are all mine. I love You Jesus and I will follow You from this moment forward till I am with You in Heaven forever! Please use me to help others know You dear LORD. In Jesus' Name, Amen.

——— • ———

Tell another Christian that Jesus has saved you into His kingdom! Find a group of Christ-loving, Bible-living believers. Be water baptized. Read your King James Bible, daily, and talk with God in prayer. Follow Christ to the end of your life.

- Give Him thanks—preferably with uplifted heart and hands, give verbal thanksgiving to the LORD daily for finding and saving you from sin and hell and for His glory and eternal purpose.
- Ask the LORD to fill you with His Holy Spirit and use you (Acts 1:48; 2:14; 2:38-39; 19:1-6).
- Tell another Christian that the LORD has saved you (Luke 12:8 -9).
- Find a group of Christ-centered believers who love God's Word and study it unceasingly. Stay clear of those who are proud of their church, their pastor, or their denomination. Fellowship with those who unceasingly magnify Jesus Christ, the nail-scarred risen Savior above all else (Colossians 2).
- Be water baptized (Acts 2:38).
- Obtain a copy of the booklet titled:

What Next? Now that You are Saved (at SafeGuardYourSoul.com or Amazon.com)

- Read your King James Bible daily and talk with God in prayer. Read at least four chapters every morning as soon as you awake. Have a Bible reading and feeding plan.
- Follow Christ to the end of your life (Matthew 24:13).
- Read and obey God's Word (James 1:22).

• You are invited to read posts, listen to audios and radio programs, etc., and sign up for the free email devotional. All of which are available at SafeGuardYourSoul.com, to help you to grow in grace as a born again disciple of Jesus (Colossians 2:6-10).

Sharpen your personal discernment. Let's grow in His grace together!

Sign up here to receive edifying emails from SafeGuardYourSoul.com.

Sign up at: **info@SafeGuardYourSoul.com**

Mailing Address:

Todd Tomasella
9201 Warren Pkwy. Ste. 200
Frisco, Texas 75035

Made in United States
Troutdale, OR
08/03/2024